JESUS THE WORD

according to John the Sectarian

JESUS THE WORD

according to John the Sectarian

*A Paleofundamentalist Manifesto
for Contemporary Evangelicalism,
Especially Its Elites,
in North America*

ROBERT H. GUNDRY

WILLIAM B. EERDMANS PUBLISHING COMPANY
GRAND RAPIDS, MICHIGAN / CAMBRIDGE, U.K.

Wm. B. Eerdmans Publishing Co.
255 Jefferson Ave. S.E., Grand Rapids, Michigan 49503 /
P.O. Box 163, Cambridge CB3 9PU U.K.

Printed in the United States of America

06 05 04 03 02   7 6 5 4 3 2 1

Library of Congress Cataloging-in-Publication Data

Gundry, Robert Horton.
Jesus the Word according to John the sectarian : a paleofundamentalist
manifesto for contemporary evangelicalism, especially
its elites, in North America / Robert H. Gundry.
p.   cm.
Includes bibliographical references.
ISBN 0-8028-4980-6 (pbk. : alk. paper)
1. Bible. N.T. John — Socio-rhetorical criticism.
2. Logos (Christian theology) — History of doctrines — Early church, ca. 30-600.
3. Jesus Christ — Person and offices — History of doctrines —
Early church, ca. 30-600. I. Title: Jesus the Word. II. Title.

BS2615.52.G86 2002
226.5'06 — dc21
2001040680

www.eerdmans.com

To Kevin J. Vanhoozer, a former student of mine, in small repayment but with large appreciation for the dedication to me of his important book, *Is There a Meaning in This Text? The Bible, the Reader, and the Morality of Literary Knowledge* (Grand Rapids, Mich.: Zondervan, 1998). For criticisms and suggestions, my thanks to Lisa DeBoer, Gaston Espinosa, Bruce Fisk, Stan Gaede, Stanley Gundry, Judith Gundry-Volf, Karen Jobes, Tremper Longman III, Jon Pott, Moisés Silva, and Jonathan Wilson.

Contents

Abbreviations   ix

foreWord   xiii

1. Jesus the Word according to John   1

2. The Sectarian   51

3. A Paleofundamentalist Manifesto for Contemporary
   Evangelicalism, Especially Its Elites, in North America   71

   A Postscript on Some Theological Desiderata   95

   Extended Endnotes   97

   The Transfiguration of Jesus according to John:
      Jesus as the Heard Word   97

   In Defense of "Exegesis" in John 1:18   98

   Angelomorphic Christology in Revelation 10:
      A Backup for the Same in John 1:51   101

CONTENTS

*Tension with the World as a Distinguishing Feature
of Sectarianism*   103

The Restriction of Love to Fellow Believers in First John   105

*Questions about the Sociological Causes of John's
Alienation from the World and about
Anti-Semitism in John*   106

*Exclusivism, Inclusivism, and Universalism in
Relation to John's Gospel*   108

The Sectarian Start of Christianity   110

Bibliography   115

Abbreviations

AB	Anchor Bible
ABRL	Anchor Bible Reference Library
ACNT	Augsburg Commentaries on the New Testament
AGJU	Arbeiten zur Geschichte des antiken Judentums und des Urchristentums
AnBib	Analecta biblica
BBB	Bonner biblische Beiträge
BBR	*Bulletin for Biblical Research*
BDB	Brown, F., S. R. Driver, and C. A. Briggs. *A Hebrew and English Lexicon of the Old Testament.* Oxford: Clarendon, 1907
BETL	Bibliotheca ephemeridum theologicarum lovaniensium
Bib	*Biblica*
BJRL	*Bulletin of the John Rylands University Library of Manchester*
BJS	Brown Judaic Studies
BZNW	Beihefte zur Zeitschrift für die neutestamentliche Wissenschaft
ConBNT	Coniectanea neotestamentica or Coniectanea biblica: New Testament Series
CTM	*Concordia Theological Monthly*
EBib	*Études bibliques*
EstBib	*Estudios biblicos*

ETL	*Ephemerides theologicae lovanienses*
ETS	Erfurter theologische Studien
EvQ	*Evangelical Quarterly*
ExpTim	*Expository Times*
GNT	Grundrisse zum Neuen Testament
HBT	*Horizons in Biblical Theology*
HKNT	Handkommentar zum Neuen Testament
HTR	*Harvard Theological Review*
JAAR	*Journal of the American Academy of Religion*
JBL	*Journal of Biblical Literature*
JSNT	*Journal for the Study of the New Testament*
JSNTSup	Journal for the Study of the New Testament: Supplement Series
JTS	*Journal of Theological Studies*
JTSA	*Journal of Theology for Southern Africa*
L&N	*Greek-English Lexicon of the New Testament: Based on Semantic Domains.* Edited by J. P. Louw and E. A. Nida. 2 vols. 2d ed. New York: United Bible Societies, 1989
LSJ	Liddell, Henry George, Robert Scott, and Henry Stuart Jones. *A Greek-English Lexicon.* 9th ed. with a revised supplement. Oxford: Clarendon, 1996
NCB	New Century Bible
NovT	*Novum Testamentum*
NovTSup	Supplements to Novum Testamentum
NTAbh	Neutestamentliche Abhandlungen
NTD	Das Neue Testament Deutsch
NTOA	Novum Testamentum et Orbis Antiquus
NTS	*New Testament Studies*
NTTS	New Testament Tools and Studies
OBO	Orbis biblicus et orientalis
RSR	*Recherches de science religieuse*
RTR	*Reformed Theological Review*
SBL	Society of Biblical Literature
SBLDS	Society of Biblical Literature Dissertation Series
SBLSBS	Society of Biblical Literature Sources for Biblical Study
SBLSP	*Society of Biblical Literature Seminar Papers*
SBLSymS	Society of Biblical Literature Symposium Series

SNTSMS   Society for New Testament Studies Monograph Series
SP   Sacra pagina
TDNT   *Theological Dictionary of the New Testament.* Edited by
          G. Kittel and G. Friedrich. Translated by G. W. Bromiley. 10
          vols. Grand Rapids, Mich.: Eerdmans, 1964-1976
TLNT   Ceslas Spicq. *Theological Lexicon of the New Testament.* Trans-
          lated and edited by James D. Ernest. 3 vols. Peabody, Mass.:
          Hendrickson, 1994
TynBul *Tyndale Bulletin*
TZ   *Theologische Zeitschrift*
WBC   Word Biblical Commentary
WTJ   *Westminster Theological Journal*
WUNT   Wissenschaftliche Untersuchungen zum Neuen Testament
ZNW   *Zeitschrift für die neutestamentliche Wissenschaft und die Kunde
          der älteren Kirche*
ZTK   *Zeitschrift für Theologie und Kirche*

fore Word

The Gospel of John starts with a foreWord, so to speak. "In the beginning" — there we have "fore." "Was the Word" — there we have "Word." What sort of Word do we hear in this Gospel, then? We hear a divine person who fore- or preexisted all things in the created order. We hear also a human person, Jesus, who in an endless stream of words speaks as the incarnate Word about himself, i.e. speaks about the Word in self-imaging words. The first chapter of the present book will spell out the ways in which these words express the Word that Jesus is.

But we must deal not only with what sort of Word Jesus is. We must also deal with what sort of author has portrayed Jesus as the Word. This portrayal of Jesus says something about John the author as well as about Jesus his subject, just as we can tell something about artists by the way they paint their subjects. The Word that John portrays — and by so doing portrays himself indirectly — this Word is one of unqualified universality notwithstanding a local setting; of imperious dogmatism notwithstanding wholesale rejection; and of antiworldliness notwithstanding enmeshment in the world. So John reveals himself to be a sectarian; for sectarianism consists in a constellation of such characteristics, as the second chapter will show.

Why should anyone pay attention to John's sectarian portrayal of Jesus the Word? I write as an evangelical Christian living in North America and observing along with others, both evangelical and nonevangelical, the current state and trajectory of evangelicalism on this land mass. Like their fundamentalist ancestors, evangelicals have wanted to preserve and propagate the biblical tenets of historic Christian faith and a corresponding lifestyle. Yet many observers of North American evangelicalism have noticed in it a recent deterioration of those tenets and that lifestyle. The deterioration seems especially noticeable when it comes to evangelical elites — the well educated, the cultured, the economically and socially upscale. Given the accuracy of this observation and our traditional appeal to the Bible, we evangelicals above all others should pay attention; for it is attention to John's sectarian portrayal of Jesus the Word which holds a possibility of rehabilitating the fundamentals of our heritage. The third chapter will detail the mentioned deterioration and poultice it with that portrayal.

I have just now referred to the fundamentals of our evangelical heritage. Enter paleofundamentalism, which carries a double connotation: first, the fundamentalism out of which grew North American evangelicalism and, second, the fundamentalism of John's sectarian portrayal of Jesus the Word. "Paleo-" alludes quite obviously to the first-century, Johannine version, and not so obviously to the world-engaged version of fundamentalism that arose early in the twentieth century but is to be distinguished from the reclusive version into which it had evolved by mid-century. Here some might ask, "Why should evangelical Christians revert to fundamentalism? Should we not, on the contrary, rejoice over having outgrown the excesses and faults of our fundamentalist adolescence? Broken out of our anti-intellectual cocoon? Reentered the mainstream? Begun to make our mark on the surrounding culture once again?" But those who might ask such questions should note the qualification "paleo-" and its double connotation, and perchance hold their questions in abeyance.

As to the further possible questions, "How dare you use John's Gospel to make your point? You call him a sectarian, but are not sectarians the most narrow-minded of fundamentalists? How could a sectarian write, as John did, 'For God so loved the world'? Does it not border on the outrageous to treat the Fourth Gospel as a manifesto for turning the

clock of evangelicalism back into a dark age we would all like to forget?"
— well, keep reading. I will address those questions head-on.

One might infer from the foregoing that I started to write this
book out of disturbance over seeing that North American evangelicalism is on the downgrade, and accelerating. But the inference would be
wrong. The book had a biblical genesis, appropriately in view of its di-
gested form as the Annual Lecture for the Thirtieth Anniversary Meeting of the Institute for Biblical Research (November 17, 2000, in Nashville, Tennessee).

More specifically, a couple of years ago I was listening to a tirade
against propositional truth under the wornout slogan, "Truth is personal,
not propositional," as though the personal cancels out the propositional.
The tirade got so annoying that a naughty thought sprang to mind:
maybe the New Living Translation, given as it is to dynamic equivalence
(the theory that translators should strive for equivalence of impact as well
as of meaning), should render John 1:1, "In the beginning was the Proposition." After all, the Greek word λόγος, traditionally translated "Word,"
does not usually refer to a single word, as the traditional English translation usually does; rather, to a set of words having a subject and a predicate, i.e. to a proposition or, more expansively, to a whole set of proposi-
tions, a discourse.

"Proposition" seemed to satisfy the criterion of equivalence in
meaning, but I wondered whether it would strike readers of the New
Living Translation as dynamic. Too humdrum, I thought. Maybe too
stilted and cerebral as well. Other possibilities offered themselves — not
only "In the beginning was the Discourse," but also "In the beginning
was the Sentence," ". . . the Statement," ". . . the Declaration," ". . . the
Speech" — but they all seemed just as humdrum as "Proposition." So I
settled back on "Word" without ever having looked to see what the New
Living Translation has actually done with λόγος in John 1:1. (I still have
not.)

My failed attempt at dynamic equivalence did set me thinking,
however, about the word "Word" in the Prologue of John's Gospel.
Since λόγος means the verbal expression of thought, it began seeming
appropriate for me to express in words my own thoughts about John's

portrayal of Jesus as the Word who himself expressed in words the thoughts of God.[1] Then there dawned on me the pertinence of that portrayal to current conditions and trends. I checked my assessments against sociological as well as theological literature, and the present book emerged.

I will bypass possibilities of conceptual background for John's use of λόγος for Jesus as the Word: possibilities such as the word of the Lord in the OT; the use of *memra*, "word," in the Targums (ancient paraphrases of the Hebrew OT in the Aramaic language); the Torah, "law, instruction," in rabbinic literature; the word of the gospel in the NT outside John; the philosophical use of λόγος by Stoics and Philo, a Jewish philosopher in first-century Alexandria; and, most prominent of all, wisdom as increasingly personified and hypostatized in Jewish literature from the OT period onward.[2] I will also bypass possibilities of a literary background for John's Prologue, which introduces Jesus as the Word: possibilities such as a Christian hymn or poem composed earlier than the writing of the Fourth Gospel, and a heretical or non-Christian hymn or poem. You can find discussions of these possible backgrounds in major commentaries on John and in many journal articles.

Other questions occupy me: Does Word-Christology disappear in John's Gospel after the Prologue? If not, how does John develop that Christology after the Prologue, and to what extent? In what frame of mind? On what ideological platform? With what practical ramifications for him and his Christian audience in relation to their environment — and for us?

To answer these questions I will engage in a christological exegesis of relevant Johannine texts, explore the sociological implications of these texts and related features of John's Gospel, and apply the findings to contemporary evangelicalism in North America, with some particular emphasis on its "knowledge industry." A short list of remaining theological

1. Cf. C. H. Dodd, *How to Read the Gospels* (Westminster, U.K.: Church Information Board, 1956), 22-23: "The Word of God is His Thought (if we may put it so) uttered so that men can understand it."

2. But for another suggestion, see the extended endnote below, "The Transfiguration of Jesus according to John: Jesus as the Heard Word."

questions will follow, plus a batch of extended endnotes whose length and tangentiality make impracticable, perhaps inappropriate, their inclusion among the footnotes. A closing bibliography will help anyone wanting to check references and hunt down materials.[3]

3. Unfortunately, Saeed Hamid-Khani's *Revelation and Concealment of Christ: A Theological Inquiry into the Elusive Language of the Fourth Gospel* (WUNT 2/120; Tübingen: Mohr Siebeck, 2000) did not reach me till too late for inclusion in the present discussion. Though he vigorously rejects a description of John as sectarian (see his pp. 174-219), I have discovered no arguments of his that my book does not address. Moreover, his rejection is limited in its engagement both with sociological literature and with the sectarian traits of John's text.

CHAPTER I

Jesus the Word According to John

I n the late nineteenth century Adolf Harnack argued for John's Prologue as a secondary addition to the rest of the Gospel, for the Prologue as designed to prepare a Hellenistic audience for the rest, and for
the rest as containing nothing of the Prologue's Word-Christology.[1] In-
versely, M.-J. Lagrange argued that the rest of John was not written in
view of the Prologue.[2] Perhaps John A. T. Robinson represented this position most prominently in more recent times: "It has been said by no less a
Johannine scholar than E. F. Scott that 'in the Fourth Gospel the Messianic idea is replaced by that of the Logos'. But this is precisely what does
not happen. The word λόγος never recurs as a title, and the dominant
christology of the Gospel is expressed rather in terms of 'the Christ, the
Son of God' (20.21)." Thus the Prologue consists of a late addition,
though Robinson detects within it, specifically in vv. 6-9, 15, the original
beginning of the Gospel.[3]

---

1. Adolf Harnack, "Ueber das Verhältnis des Prologs des vierten Evangeliums
zum ganzen Werk," *ZTK* 2 (1892): 189-231, esp. 230-31.
2. M.-J. Lagrange, *Évangile selon Saint Jean* (5th ed.; EBib; Paris: Gabalda,
1936), CLXX.
3. John A. T. Robinson, *Twelve More New Testament Studies* (London: SCM,
1984), 65-76, esp. 69 for the quotation; cf. C. H. Dodd, *The Interpretation of the
Fourth Gospel* (Cambridge: Cambridge University Press, 1960), 292-96; Barnabas

Robinson acknowledged thematic interrelations between the Prologue and the rest of John. The themes include the preexistence of Christ, the contrast between light and darkness, the seeing of Jesus' glory, the seeing of God by no one except Jesus, etc. But in the Prologue such themes reflect the rest of the Gospel, written earlier; and since in Robinson's view the rest contains no Word-Christology, this Christology injects into the Prologue, written later, something new and unrelated.

On the ground of those themes that the Prologue and the rest of John do share, plus similarities of vocabulary and style, other scholars deny a late addition of the Prologue, but with Harnack, Lagrange, and Robinson see no Word-Christology in the rest of the Gospel.[4] Still other scholars think not only that whatever its background the Prologue belonged to the original version of John, but also that the Word in the Prologue "gives expression to the idea of revelation which dominates the whole Gospel."[5] Thus, the portrayal of Jesus as the Word in John's Prologue works itself out in an emphasis on Jesus' word, or words, in the rest of the Gospel. Rudolf Bultmann developed this view theologically, and Ed. L. Miller has developed it historicocritically by exposing the weak-

---

Lindars, *Behind the Fourth Gospel* (Studies in Creative Criticism 3; London: SPCK, 1971), 74; John Ashton, *Understanding the Fourth Gospel* (Oxford: Clarendon, 1991), 345n.27.

4. See, e.g., James D. G. Dunn, "Let John Be John: A Gospel for Its Time," in *The Gospel and the Gospels* (ed. P. Stuhlmacher; Grand Rapids, Mich.: Eerdmans, 1991), 313n.78: "I find it impossible to regard the prologue of John's Gospel as redactional (i.e., added after the evangelist put the Gospel into its present form); the themes of the prologue are too closely integrated into the Gospel as a whole and are so clearly intended to introduce these themes that such a conclusion is rendered implausible." But except in dependence on Wisdom-Christology, Word-Christology makes no appearance in Dunn's list and discussion of these common themes (pp. 314-17). Cf. John Painter, "Inclined to God: The Quest for Eternal Life — Bultmannian Hermeneutics and the Theology of the Fourth Gospel," in *Exploring the Gospel of John* (ed. R. Alan Culpepper and C. Clifton Black; Louisville, Ky.: Westminster John Knox, 1996), 348: "this use of the Logos [as giving 'expression to the theme of revelation'] is restricted to the prologue."

5. Rudolf Bultmann, *The Gospel of John: A Commentary* (ed. R. W. N. Hoare and J. K. Riches; trans. G. R. Beasley-Murray; Oxford: Blackwell, 1971), 13n.1.

nesses of standard views concerning the origin of Word-Christology and by substituting the informal emphasis on Jesus' words in the rest of the Gospel as grist for the mill that ground out the formal concept of Jesus as the Word.[6]

I will try to show that a Christology of the Word dominates the whole of John's Gospel more than has been recognized before; that this domination makes the Gospel a totalizing narrative; that in conjunction with corresponding features of John the totalizing character of this narrative exhibits strong sectarianism; and that current trends in North American evangelicalism call for a strong dose of John's logocentric sectarianism.

To discover the pervasiveness of Word-Christology and simultaneously pay due to the authority of Scripture in its final form, let us adopt the synchronic approach, take John's text as it presently stands, and use the Prologue to illuminate the rest in respect to Jesus' words. For whether or not John wrote his Prologue last and prefixed it to the rest, the Prologue comes first in the text and therefore casts the later words of Jesus in the light of Word-Christology.[7] As a result his words appear, not as the

6. Ed. L. Miller, "The Johannine Origins of the Johannine Logos," *JBL* 112 (1993): 445-57. Yet Miller countenances the possibility, it should be added, that the association of λόγος with σοφία exercised some influence on the choice of λόγος over ῥῆμα, another Greek word that John often uses in the plural for Jesus' words. Against an origin in hypostatized Wisdom we might ask why John never uses the feminine noun σοφία, "wisdom," for Jesus alongside the masculine λόγος despite John's famous fondness for synonyms and despite his frequent use of other feminine nouns for Jesus: θύρα, "door," ὁδός, "way," ἀλήθεια, "truth," ἀνάστασις, "resurrection," ζωή, "life," and ἄμπελος, "vine" (John 10:7, 9; 11:25; 14:6; 15:1, 5). Cf. Werner H. Kelber, "The Authority of the Word in St. John's Gospel: Charismatic Speech, Narrative Text, Logocentric Metaphysics," *Oral Tradition* 2 (1987): 109; and contrast with John's disuse of σοφία, the use of σοφία for Jesus in Matt 11:19 with 11:2 (par. Luke 7:35); 1 Cor 1:24, 30.

7. Cf. Jean Zumstein ("Le prologue, seuil du Quatrième Évangile," *RSR* 83 [1995]: 225-34), who assigns John's Prologue to "le genre littéraire du prédiscours": "Le prologue est donc un prédiscours dont la fonction consiste à diriger la lecture, à contrôler le décodage du récit, à prévenir les interprétations erronées" (p. 228). Zumstein misses the extension of Word-Christology past the Prologue into the rest of John's Gospel, however. My adoption of the synchronic approach denies neither the validity of a diachronic approach, such as is used in source criticism and redaction

soil out of which grew Word-Christology, but as the fruit, the outworking in Jesus' earthly ministry, of Word-Christology. At least for the audience of the Fourth Gospel, if not for its author, Word-Christology is cause rather than effect, not vice versa. Perhaps so for the author as well, for what else would have prompted him to put so much emphasis on Jesus' words (an emphasis we are about to delineate)? Yet we can think of a number of possibilities other than that emphasis for the prompting of Word-Christology, hypostatized Wisdom being the current favorite, though whether we should regard Word-Christology as pro-Wisdom or anti-Wisdom poses yet another question.[8]

To the business of delineating John's emphasis on the words of Jesus — first, their volume. Following the Prologue we have what someone has called a "sheer avalanche" of them, so that Frank Kermode has described the Johannine Jesus as "by far the most communicative of the four [Jesuses portrayed in the canonical gospels]."[9] Jesus' speech occupies vast stretches

---

criticism, nor the possibility that a diachronic approach proves useful when applied to John. That it does prove useful is debatable, however.

8. For just two of many possible examples of a positive attitude toward Wisdom, see Ben Witherington III, *John's Wisdom: A Commentary on the Fourth Gospel* (Louisville, Ky.: Westminster John Knox, 1995), and Martin Scott, *Sophia and the Johannine Jesus* (JSNTSup 71; Sheffield: Sheffield Academic Press, 1992). Scott argues that Wisdom, i.e. Sophia, was so thoroughly female in the way she was presented throughout the ancient Near East (he even introduces as background various goddesses) that in view of Jesus' maleness John shifted to the masculine noun λόγος. On the other hand, Scott continues, "because it [the Logos] is merely a vehicle accomodating [*sic*] the introduction of Jesus Sophia, whose progress is then mapped throughout the Gospel, it is immediately dispensable" (p. 173). We are in the process of discovering that by no means does John dispense with the Logos after the Prologue. For an example of negativity toward Wisdom, see Norman R. Petersen, *The Gospel of John and the Sociology of Light: Language and Characterization in the Fourth Gospel* (Valley Forge, Pa.: Trinity Press International, 1993), 110-32. Along the same line, Karen H. Jobes ("Sophia Christology: The Way of Wisdom?" in *The Way of Wisdom: Essays in Honor of Bruce K. Waltke* [ed. J. I. Packer and Sven K. Soderlund; Grand Rapids, Mich.: Zondervan, 2000], 226-50) calls attention to distinctions in Jewish wisdom tradition which undercut the supposition that John was drawing on a unified tradition.

9. Frank Kermode, "John," in *The Literary Guide to the Bible* (ed. Robert Alter and Frank Kermode; Cambridge, Mass.: Harvard University Press, 1987), 453.

of John's text. After discounting chapter 21 as a redactional addition, Werner H. Kelber calculates that about four-fifths of chapters 1–17 and about three-fourths of chapters 1–20 consist of Jesus' sayings, dialogues, and monologues.[10] The addition of chapter 21 would not reduce that figure appreciably. We can see the emphasis on Jesus' words most clearly in comparisons with synoptic parallels. John adds to the feeding of the five thousand Jesus' long discourse on the bread of life (6:26-66). The Synoptics have nothing of the sort, though they all narrate the feeding. Similarly, John adds to the triumphal entry, also narrated in the Synoptics, Jesus' discourse on his death like that of a grain of wheat (12:20-36, 44-50). Even more extensively, in John the few words of Jesus at the Last Supper according to the Synoptics balloon into almost four whole chapters (13–16). A chapter-long prayer (17) replaces his short prayers in Gethsemane according to the Synoptics. And though John inserts no discourse into the passion narrative, his Jesus certainly speaks a lot more than the synoptic Jesus does, particularly during Jesus' trial. John's Jesus is a lamb (1:29, 36), but no lamb dumb before his shearers, as mostly in the Synoptics.

To make room for Jesus' added speech, John has greatly reduced both the volume and the number of narratives concerning Jesus' deeds. This reduction comes despite an emphasis on Jesus' "works," which John also calls "signs." Of 666 verses in Mark, according to Gary M. Burge, 209 (= 31%) deal with Jesus' miracles. If the passion narrative is left out of account, 200 verses out of 425 (= 47%) do. Matthew and Luke tend to add to the number of miracles in Mark. But John, though he knows of more and says so (20:30-31; 21:25), narrates only seven and treats them (I might add) not as "miracles" (i.e. "acts of power") to be admired but as the aforementioned "works" and "signs" to be explained by Jesus' words, so that the works and signs turn into *verba visibilia*.[11]

10. Werner H. Kelber, "The Authority of the Word in St. John's Gospel," 110-11; idem, "Die Fleischwerdung des Wortes in der Körperlichkeit des Textes," in *Materialität der Kommunikation* (ed. Hans Ulrich Gumbrecht and K. Ludwig Pfeiffer; Suhrkamp Taschenbuch Wissenschaft 70; Frankfurt am Main: Suhrkamp, 1988), 33-34; idem, "In the Beginning Were the Words: The Apotheosis and Narrative Displacement of the Logos," *JAAR* 58 (1990): 82.

11. For the statistics, see Gary M. Burge, *The Anointed Community: The Holy*

But we have in John not just a huge proportion of Jesus' words. John continually takes pains to highlight Jesus' words qua words. Here we must bring in John's use of ῥήματα, "words," alongside λόγος. Always in the plural, ῥήματα occurs nine times for Jesus' words[12] and three times for the words of God that Jesus speaks,[13] so that the references to Jesus' ῥήματα are to be understood as also the ῥήματα of God. Outside the Prologue John uses λόγος three times in the plural for Jesus' words,[14] but eighteen times in the singular for Jesus' word,[15] six times in the singular for God's word,[16] and twice in the singular for the word of God that Jesus speaks,[17] so that as in the case of ῥήματα, the λόγος and λόγοι of Jesus are to be understood as also those of God. Naturally, the predominant singular of λόγος recalls the initial portrayal of Jesus as the Word (singular).[18]

The Synoptics barely call attention to Jesus' λόγοι, only twice in Mark, four times in Matthew, and three times in Luke, and only in the plural, never in the singular.[19] ῥῆμα fares slightly better in the Synoptics,

---

Spirit in the Johannine Tradition (Grand Rapids, Mich.: Eerdmans, 1987), 74-78; and for the works and signs as "visible words," see Rudolf Bultmann, *Theology of the New Testament* (trans. Kendrick Grobel; 2 vols.; New York: Scribner's, 1955), 2:60; cf. idem, *John,* 163: "If in Jesus the λόγος became flesh, then God's action is carried out in Jesus' words." Bultmann errs, however, in collapsing works into words. One is reminded that Goethe's Faust translated John 1:1, "In the beginning was the Deed [*Tat,* a possible translation for ἔργον, which John uses for Jesus' works]." More pertinent is that the Hebrew דבר means deed as well as word.

12. John 5:47; 6:63, 68; 8:20; 10:21; 12:47, 48; 14:10; 15:7.

13. John 3:34; 8:47; 17:8.

14. John 7:40; 10:19; 14:24.

15. John 2:22; 4:41, 50; 5:24; 6:60; 7:36; 8:31, 37, 43, 51, 52; 12:48; 14:23; 15:3, 20 (*bis*); 18:9, 32. These occurrences are divided almost evenly between Jesus' message in general and particular sayings of Jesus. Even in the case of his particular sayings, the point remains that John calls attention to Jesus' word to a degree far from matched in the Synoptics.

16. John 5:38; 8:55; 10:35; 17:6, 14, 17.

17. John 14:24; 17:14.

18. John 1:1 (*tris*), 14.

19. Mark 8:38 (par. Luke 9:26); 13:31 (par. Matt 24:35 and Luke 21:33); Matt 7:24 (par. Luke 6:47), 26, 28.

where it occurs for Jesus' words in Luke twice in the plural[20] and in the singular twice in Mark, once in Matthew, and eight times in Luke as never in John.[21] It appears that John has gone far out of his way to multiply references to Jesus' words qua words — there are almost twice as many occurrences of these terms in John as in all three Synoptics put together, almost three times as many if we count paralleled occurrences in the Synoptics once each — and to concentrate them primarily into the singular of λόγος and thus line them up with Jesus the λόγος. The words that Jesus speaks, he speaks as the Word; and since he speaks as the Word, the plurality of his words constitutes the singularity of his word, a reminder of who he is. And since as the Word he was with God in the beginning, and was God, his word is at one and the same time God's word. Thus the rest of the Fourth Gospel dovetails with the Prologue.

The synonymity of the singular and plural of λόγος is evident in John 14:24: "The one not loving me does not keep my *words*, and the *word* which you hear is not mine, but [is the word] of the Father who sent me." The synonymity of the singular of λόγος with the plural of ῥῆμα is evident in John 8:47, 51-52: "The one who is of God hears the *words* of God. . . . if anyone keeps my *word* . . . . if anyone keeps my *word*" (cf. 3:34: "for he whom God sent speaks the *words* of God"); 12:48: "The one . . . not receiving my *words* has the one judging him; the *word* that I spoke — that will judge him at the last day"; 15:3, 7: "Already you are clean on account of the *word* that I have spoken to you. . . . If you abide in me and my *words* abide in you . . ."; and 17:6, 8, 14, 17: "they have kept your *word*. . . . the *words* that you gave me I have given them. . . . I have given them your *word*. . . . Your *word* is truth."[22] F.-M. Braun devotes a whole article to the synonymity of singular and plural expressions in John,[23] and

20. Luke 7:1; 24:8.

21. Mark 9:32 (par. Luke 9:45); 14:72 (par. Matt 26:75 and Luke 22:61); Luke 2:50; 5:5; 9:45 (*bis*); 18:34; 20:26.

22. Cf. Alf Corell, *Consummatum Est: Eschatology and Church in the Gospel of St. John* (London: SPCK, 1958), 119-22; Ignace de la Potterie, *La vérité dans Saint Jean* (2 vols.; AnBib 73-74; Rome: Biblical Institute Press, 1977), 1:43-44; G. Kittel, "λέγω, λόγος, κτλ," *TDNT* 4:105-6.

23. F.-M. Braun, "La Réduction du Pluriel au Singulier dans l'Évangile et la

John's penchant for using synonyms is too well known to need very much detailing.[24]

The synonymous use of λόγος, λόγοι, and ῥήματα has enjoyed wide recognition. Comparatively unrecognized is John's frequent and synonymous use of ἐντολή(-αί), "commandment(s)," as in 14:15, 21; 15:10, 12, all of which speak of keeping Jesus' commandments, or commandment, and 8:51, 52; 14:23, 24; 15:20; 17:6, all of which speak of keeping his word (λόγον).[25] Though the verb of commanding (ἐντέλλομαι) has Jesus as its subject in Matt 17:9; 28:20, as in John 15:17, the cognate noun never occurs in the Synoptics for Jesus' words. It occurs only for OT commandments, except for Luke 15:29, where it occurs as a collective singular for the commands of the prodigal son's father. By contrast, neither the noun nor the verb ever occurs in John for OT commandments, only for Jesus' commandments and for the Father's commanding Jesus (with the sole exception of the chief priests' and Pharisees' commands in 11:57 concerning Jesus' arrest).[26]

But to appreciate adequately the wordfulness of Jesus the Word in John and the attention that John calls to it, we must expand our semantic field beyond λόγος, ῥῆμα, and ἐντολή.[27] In John's Gospel μαρτυρέω and

---

Première Lettre de Jean," *NTS* 24 (1977-78): 40-67; cf. idem, *Jean le Théologien*, vol. 2: *Les Grandes Traditions d'Israël et l'accord des Écritures d'après le Quatrième Évangile* (EBib; Paris: Gabalda, 1964), 140-41. Other examples of the synonymity of singular and plural include "commandment" and "commandments" (John 15:10-12; cf. 15:17: "These things I command you"), "work" and "works" (6:28-29), and "sin" and "sins" (8:21, 24; 15:22, 24).

24. Since we are dealing with synonymous nouns, I example κόλπος and στῆθος for "bosom" (1:18; 13:23, 25; 21:20), παιδίον, παῖς, and υἱός for "child, son" (4:46-54), ἄρτος and βρῶσις for "bread, food" (6:26-59), ὀψάριον and προσφάγιον for "fish relish" (21:1-13), and Ἰουδαῖοι and Φαρισαῖοι for Jesus' opponents (9:13-41), not to mention synonymous verbs for eating, washing, drawing, carrying, rising, sending, going, loving, and emoting as well as other sorts of expressions, such as prepositional phrases.

25. The OT uses "words" for commandments in many passages (for references see BDB s.v. דבר II 2).

26. John 10:18; 12:49, 50; 13:34; 14:15, 21, 31; 15:10, 12, 14, 17.

27. Theophil Müller (*Das Heilsgeschehen im Johannesevangelium: Eine exe-*

μαρτυρία occur sixteen times for Jesus' testimony, but never for it in the Synoptic Gospels.[28] Though the Synoptics have Jesus as the subject of φωνέω, "produce a sound, call, speak loudly," a number of times,[29] they use φωνή for Jesus' voice only in the cry of dereliction and death-cry,[30] whereas John calls attention to the voice of Jesus nine times.[31] The Word has a voice (cf. *Acts of Peter* 38 [9], where Christ is identified as "the Word stretched out [on the cross], the one and only, concerning whom the Spirit says, 'For what is Christ but the Word, the sound [ἦχος] of God?'")! To emphasize the words spoken with that voice, John doubles

---

getische Studie, zugleich der Versuch einer Antwort an Rudolf Bultmann [Frankfurt am Main: Gotthelf-Verlag, 1961], 21-22) expands the semantic field but does not go into sufficient detail.

28. See John 3:11, 32, 33; 4:44; 5:31; 7:7; 8:13, 14, 18; 13:21; 18:37. Cf. the association of testimony with "the word of God" in the Book of Revelation. There, 19:13 says that Jesus' name is "the Word of God." Therefore testifying "to the word of God" and John's exile on Patmos "because of the word of God" in 1:2, 9 probably mean testifying to Jesus himself, and exile because of him. And since in 1:2, 9; 20:4 "the testimony of Jesus (Christ)" is paired with "the Word of God," we should probably consider "the Testimony of Jesus" another christological title (cf. the pairing of "the testimony of Jesus" with "the commandments of God" in 12:17). Favoring this view are (1) the designation of Jesus as "the faithful (and true) testifier" in 1:5; 3:14 (in the latter passage with the apposition, "the beginning of God's creation" — cf. John 1:1-3); (2) the description of Jesus himself and "the words of God" as "(faithful and) true" in 3:7; 6:10; 19:9, 11 (cf. 17:17; 21:5; 22:6); (3) the pairing of his word with his name in 3:8; (4) the pairing of "the word of God" with "the testimony that they had" in 6:9; (5) the combination of "word" and "testimony" in the phrase "the word of their testimony"; (6) the pairing of that phrase with "the blood of the Lamb" in 12:11; (7) the combining of "word" and "endurance" in the phrase "my word of endurance" after "endurance" has been located "in Jesus" (1:9); and (8) the equation of "the testimony of Jesus" with "the Spirit of prophecy" in 19:10. Throughout these passages "word" goes back to λόγος.

29. Mark 9:35; 10:49; 15:35 (par. Matt 27:47); Matt 20:32; Luke 8:8, 54; 23:46.

30. Mark 15:34, 37 (par. Matt 27:46, 50 and Luke 23:46).

31. John 3:29; 5:25, 28; 10:3, 4, 16, 27; 11:43; 18:37. For more detailed contrasts between the use of φωνή in the Synoptics and in John, see F.-M. Braun, *Jean le Théologien*, vol. 3, part 1: *Sa théologie: Le mystère de Jésus-Christ* (Paris: Gabalda, 1966), 102.

the "Amen" in front of Jesus' "I say to you" no fewer than twenty-five times. The Synoptics never double the "Amen."[32] Very often φωνή, "voice," is used for "the sound of a cry or shout";[33] so it comes as no surprise that Jesus "shouts" (κράζω, κραυγάζω) several times in John,[34] as he does only in the cry of dereliction in a single one of the Synoptics.[35] He shouts in John even when he teaches,[36] as he never does when teaching in the Synoptics. We are far from the Jesus who in Matt 12:19 does not shout, and whose voice no one hears in the streets.

Though the Synoptics portray Jesus as teaching more often than John portrays him as teaching, John portrays Jesus as a rabbi (ῥαββί and ῥαββουνί) significantly more often (eight times) than the Synoptics do (Mark — five times; Matthew — two times, or three if 23:8 implies as much; Luke — none), and twice takes care to translate the term with "Teacher."[37] Only in John, moreover, does Jesus repeatedly describe his teaching as God's, which description reminds one of the Prologue's Word who was with God and was God.[38] Thus the Word will publicly make an-

32. Cf. Boy Hinrichs, *"Ich Bin": Die Konsistenz des Johannes-Evangeliums in der Konzentration auf des Wort Jesu* (Stuttgarter Bibelstudien 133; Stuttgart: Katholisches Bibelwerk, 1988), 31. A. J. B. Higgins ("The Words of Jesus according to St. John," *BJRL* 49 [1966-67]: 371-72) suggests that the double preliminary "Amen" in John "corresponds to a variation from the single 'amen' in Jesus' own speech," but Higgins offers no evidence or argument that Jesus himself doubled the preliminary "Amen."

33. L&N 1:398 §33.80; cf. Elizabeth Harris, *Prologue and Gospel: The Theology of the Fourth Evangelist* (JSNTSup 107; Sheffield: Sheffield Academic Press, 1994), 35, on the use of κράζω as an emphatic verb that introduces "solemn, oracular utterances," and A. E. Harvey, *Jesus on Trial: A Study in the Fourth Gospel* (Atlanta: John Knox, 1977), 23-24, on its forensic use, with which we might compare the testifying of Jesus in John.

34. John 7:28, 37; 11:43; 12:44.

35. Matt 27:50.

36. John 7:28.

37. Cf. Andreas J. Köstenberger, "Jesus as Rabbi in the Fourth Gospel," *BBR* 8 (1998): 97-128, esp. 112-15. Whereas I am arguing for a theological point — viz., the pervasiveness of the Word as a wordsmith throughout John — Köstenberger argues for the historicity of Johannine tradition.

38. John 6:44-46; 7:14-17; 8:28.

nouncement (ἀπαγγελῶ) concerning the Father,[39] and has exegeted (ἐξηγήσατο) him.[40]

In John Jesus appears as a prophet, the scriptural connotation of which is a conveyor of God's word, almost as many times (six) as he does in Luke (seven, as against three times each in Mark and Matthew). Though the portrayal of Jesus as a prophet falls below a high Christology, we should not discount it; for Jesus portrays himself as such — and if anyone in the Gospels counts as a reliable character, he does.[41] Though the comparative statistics on λέγω, "say," are unenlightening,[42] as also those on φημί, "say,"[43] the statistics on λαλέω, "speak," and λαλιά, "speech," speak volumes. Of their sixty-one occurrences in John, fifty have to do with Jesus' speaking, as compared with only nine such occurrences in Mark, twelve in Matthew, and ten in Luke. And as in the case of Jesus' teaching, John repeatedly describes Jesus' speaking (λαλέω) as God's ("I do not speak [λαλῶ] from myself" — John 14:10),[44] and in 8:43 he couples Jesus' speech (λαλιάν) with Jesus' word (λόγον).

Again it does not surprise us to learn that John refers eleven times to hearing Jesus' word, words, and voice,[45] over against four such references in Mark,[46] eight in Matthew,[47] and four, possibly only two, in Luke.[48] More impressively, John refers to believing Jesus' word, or words,[49] and to

39. John 16:25: ἀλλὰ παρρησίᾳ περὶ τοῦ πατρὸς ἀπαγγελῶ ὑμῖν.

40. John 1:18: ἐκεῖνος ἐξηγήσατο.

41. John 4:44; Mark 6:4; Matt 13:57; Luke 4:24; 13:33. Cf. Adele Reinhartz, "Jesus as Prophet: Predictive Prolepses in the Fourth Gospel," *JSNT* 36 (1989): 3-16. She traces through John the theme of Jesus as a prophet whose predictions have come to pass and thus support the divine origin of his words and his deity.

42. Matthew — 475x; Mark — 289x; Luke — 515x; John — 474x.

43. Matthew — 16x; Mark — 6x; Luke — 8x; John — 25x.

44. See also 3:10-13, 34; 7:16-18; 8:25-30, 38, 40, 42-44; 12:48-50; 16:25 (?); 17:13-14; cf. 16:13.

45. John 5:24, 25, 28; 7:40; 8:43; 10:3, 16, 27; 12:47; 14:24; 18:37.

46. Mark 4:15, 16, 18, 20.

47. Matt 7:24, 26; 13:19, 20, 22, 23; 15:12; 19:22.

48. Luke 6:47; 8:8, 15; 10:39, though in view of "the word *of God*" in 8:21 we may need to subtract 8:8, 15.

49. John 2:22; 4:50; 5:47; cf. 3:12; 10:25; 12:38.

abiding in Jesus' word and its abiding in the disciples, as the Synoptics never do.[50] Matthew refers once to keeping whatever Jesus has commanded, but John refers eight times to keeping Jesus' commands, word, and words (not so at all in Mark and Luke).[51]

But enough of semantic fields, synonyms, and statistics. Let us go to individual texts. According to what is generally considered the last verse of the Prologue, John 1:18, "A unique one, [who was] God, the one existing in the bosom of the Father — that one has exegeted (ἐξηγήσατο) [him]."[52] Exegeting the Father at the end of the Prologue forms a nice *inclusio* with the Word at the start of the Prologue in that "a unique one, [who was] God," corresponds to "the Word was God" and in that the unique one's having exegeted God indicates why the unique one is called "the Word" in relation to God. Jesus Christ was the exegetical Word of God.[53] Thus 1:18 leads into the word, words, speech, testimony, commandment, commandments, voice, and shouting of the Word.[54]

In 1:51 this exegete turns into Jacob's ladder: "you [plural: Nathaniel plus others] will see the heaven opened and the angels of God ascending and descending on the Son of Man" (cf. Jesus' calling Nathaniel "truly an Israelite" — "Israel" being Jacob's new name, of course — in 1:47). Ascending precedes descending, surprisingly in view of the reverse order in 3:13; 6:62, under the influence of Gen 28:12, the passage having to do with Jacob's ladder.[55] Since by definition angels are messengers, Jesus the ladder is a vertical information highway between an

---

50. John 5:38; 15:7.

51. Matt 28:20; John 8:51, 52; 14:15, 21, 23, 24; 15:10, 20.

52. For this reading and translation of 1:18, see Hans-Christian Kammler, *Christologie und Eschatologie: Joh 5, 17-30 als Schlüsseltext johanneischer Theologie* (WUNT 126; Tübingen: Mohr Siebeck, 2000), 113-15.

53. See further the extended endnote below, "In Defense of 'Exegesis' in John 1:18."

54. Inasmuch as ἐξηγέομαι means to tell at length, to relate in full, Francis J. Moloney (*Belief in the Word: Reading the Fourth Gospel: John 1–4* [Minneapolis: Fortress, 1993], 50) notes the transitional function of 1:18 as a lead into the following narrative (cf. Zumstein, "Le prologue," 221).

55. Cf. Anthony Tyrrell Hanson, *The Prophetic Gospel: A Study of John and the Old Testament* (Edinburgh: T&T Clark, 1991), 37.

open heaven and the earth. Elsewhere in John ascent and descent take place between heaven and earth, not within heaven, so that we should not think of the Son of Man as a ladder located up there, and of the angels' ascending and descending on him as restricted to the heavenly sphere, or of the angels as ascending to him from lower in heaven, and descending to him from higher in heaven. Unless he were in heaven and on earth at the same time (against which notion see, e.g., John 6:62, "If therefore you should see the Son of Man ascending to where he was before," and 17:11, "I am no longer in the world"), the angels' ascending from earth to him in heaven would leave their descent without him as its destination, just as their descending from heaven to him on earth would leave their ascent without him as its destination.[56] The Son of Man is not located at the bottom or the top of the ladder as the destination *to* which the angels ascend and descend. He is the ladder *on* which they ascend and descend.[57]

Whereas the Synoptics have the Son of Man seated at God's right hand and coming with the clouds of heaven and with angels as gatherers of the elect,[58] John has the Son of Man positioned as a ladder linking the open heaven to believers below, with angels acting as messengers.[59] The angels' use of this ladder resonates with the underestimated angelo-

---

56. Against Witherington (*John's Wisdom,* 72), who has the angels ascending "from" the Son of Man (so also Ernst Käsemann, *The Testament of Jesus: A Study of the Gospel of John in the Light of Chapter 17* [trans. Gerhard Krodel; Philadelphia: Fortress, 1968], 70; Rudolf Schnackenburg, *The Gospel according to St John, Volume One: Introduction and Commentary on Chapters 1–4* [trans. Kevin Smyth; Herder's Theological Commentary on the New Testament; New York: Herder, 1968], 321). But ἐπί means "on" or "to," not "from."

57. For some especially pertinent Johannine examples of ἐπί plus an accusative as indicating location rather than destination, see 1:32, 33; 3:36; 12:14, 15; 13:25; 21:20 — against Gen 28:12 LXX, which has the genitive following ἐπί, and against Christopher Rowland, "John 1. 51, Jewish Apocalyptic and Targumic Tradition," *NTS* 30 (1984): 498-507.

58. Mark 13:26-27 par. Matt 24:30-31 and Luke 21:27; Mark 14:62 par. Matt 26:64 and Luke 22:67-70.

59. Siegfried Schulz, *Untersuchungen zur Menschensohn-Christologie im Johannesevangelium: Zugleich ein Beitrag zur Methodengeschichte der Auslegung des 4. Evangeliums* (Göttingen: Vandenhoeck & Ruprecht, 1957), 102-3.

morphic Christology found in John's Gospel as well as in the Apocalypse of John,[60] where Jesus is also portrayed as "the Word of God" (Rev 19:13; cf. Philo's calling "the Word" [ὁ λόγος] God's "chief messenger" [ἀρχάγγελος] in *Her.* 42 §205). Message and messenger merge.[61]

The view of John Painter that Jesus is not Jacob's ladder, but the Son of Man enthroned in heaven by way of a ladder-like cross (in correction of Nathaniel's notion of an earthly kingship), disagrees with the angels' descending on the Son of Man. Painter's argument that no angelic mediators appear in John fails to consider the coalescence of Son of Man-Christology with angelomorphic Christology, a coalescence mediated by Word-Christology, so that the ladder and the angels ascending and descending on it are to be seen as an indivisible figure of speech referring to Jesus the Word. Apart from them as messengers the allusion to Jacob's ladder does not convey any thought of communication, for the absence of "ladder" would keep the allusion obscure and therefore God's speaking to Jacob out of the picture. The angels are just as christological as is the ladder, then. Nathaniel and his fellow disciples will see Jesus in these communicative terms throughout Jesus' earthly ministry.[62]

60. For angelomorphic Christology in John's Gospel and a bibliography of recent work along the same line by Jan-A. Bühner, Charles H. Talbert, John Ashton, and Robert Paschal, see Charles A. Gieschen, *Angelomorphic Christology: Antecedents and Early Evidence* (AGJU 42; Leiden: Brill, 1998), 18-19, 270-93. For angelomorphic Christology in the Apocalypse of John, see Robert H. Gundry, "Angelomorphic Christology in the Book of Revelation," in *SBL Seminar Papers, 1994* (SBLSP 33; Atlanta: Scholars Press, 1994), 662-78; Gieschen, *Angelomorphic Christology,* 245-69, again with bibliography; and the extended endnote below, "Angelomorphic Christology in Revelation 10: A Backup for the Same in John 1:51."

61. Cf. Stephen S. Smalley, "Johannes 1,51 und die Einleitung zum vierten Evangelium," in *Jesus und der Menschensohn* (ed. Rudolf Pesch and Rudolf Schnackenburg with Odilo Kaiser; Freiburg: Herder, 1975), 312-13: "Himmel und Erde sind in der Person Jesu, des Menschensohnes, einzigartig zusammengebracht worden, aufgrund seiner engen Beziehung zum Vater. . . . Joh 1,51 blickt auf Jesus als des Wort (Joh 1,1.14) zurück." See also Jey J. Kanagaraj, "Jesus the King, Merkabah Mysticism and the Gospel of John," *TynBul* 47 (1996): 352: "their [the angels'] movements highlight the communication that is possible between heaven and earth in Jesus."

62. Against John Painter, *Reading John's Gospel Today* (Atlanta: John Knox, 1975), 56.

The story of Jesus' first sign, the turning of water to wine, resonates with Word-Christology in the Prologue. Mary his mother tells the servants, "Do whatever he *says* (λέγει) to you" (2:5). Apparently she believes in Jesus' word, or in Jesus as the Word, even before he performs his first sign. She has read the Prologue, so to speak. Then Jesus proceeds to perform the sign by speaking. John doubles the introduction to Jesus' speaking, both times with a vivid historical present tense: (1) "And Jesus says (λέγει) to them, 'Fill the jars with water'" (2:7); "And he says (λέγει) to them, 'Draw now and carry [it] to the toastmaster'" (2:8).[63] As a result, Jesus "manifested his glory" (2:11a), previously defined as the glory of "the Word" who "became flesh and tabernacled among us" (1:14); and "his disciples believed in him" (2:11b), just as the Prologue equated those who received the Word with those who believed in his name, i.e. in him as "the Word" who has now begun to manifest his glory.[64]

In 2:22 John writes, "When therefore he [Jesus] had risen from the dead his disciples remembered that he had been saying (ἔλεγεν) this, and they believed . . . the word (τῷ λόγῳ) that Jesus had spoken (εἶπεν)." "This" refers to Jesus' word to the Jews, "Tear down this temple and in three days I will raise it" (2:19). John has interpreted this word as a statement "concerning the temple of his [Jesus'] body" (2:21), which again recalls the Word's becoming flesh and tabernacling among us (1:14). The disciples' believing Jesus' word plays again on their believing in Jesus as the Word, his name in the Prologue (1:12). And the believing of many "in his name" at 2:23 echoes yet again the Prologue's tagging Jesus with the name "Word."[65]

---

63. On John's use of the vivid historical present tense, see Jörg Frey, *Die johanneische Eschatologie*, vol. 2: *Das johanneische Zeitverständnis* (WUNT 110; Tübingen: Mohr Siebeck, 1998), 148-49.

64. See C. E. B. Cranfield, "John 1[14]: 'became,'" *ExpTim* 93 (1981-82): 215, that in John 1:14 ἐγένετο means "became" or "was made" without implication that the Word ceased to be the Word, so that the translation, "The Word came on the scene as flesh," is unnecessary. Though ἐγένετο means "came on the scene" for John the Baptist in 1:6, there it lacks a predicate nominative such as σάρξ, "flesh," in 1:14 (against C. K. Barrett, *The Gospel according to St. John: An Introduction with Commentary and Notes on the Greek Text* [2d ed.; Philadelphia: Westminster, 1978], 165).

65. On the Word as Jesus' name, cf. 1 John 5:13; 3 John 7 with 1 John 1:1 and

John 3:8 refers to the φωνήν, "sound, voice," of the πνεῦμα, "wind, Spirit." Since the wind that "blows where it wishes" is the Spirit (cf. 3:5), the wind's "sound" — i.e. the Spirit's "voice" — is Jesus. For just as Nicodemus "is hearing" (ἀκούεις) the wind, representing the Spirit, but "does not know where it is coming from and going to," so Jesus says in 8:14 that his listeners do not know where *he* has come from and where *he* is going to.[66] In other words, Jesus sets up a parallel between himself and the Spirit, whose voice he is. Thus, in 3:11 the "we" who speak (λαλοῦμεν) and the "our" whose testimony "you [plural] do not receive" (cf. the Prologue on the Word, particularly 1:11-13, in connection with not receiving versus believing and [re]birth, as here in ch. 3) — the "we" and the "our" are Jesus and the Spirit, who testify in conjunction with each other (see 8:14, 18a with 15:26 and cf. the conjunction of voice and testimony in 5:37).[67] The parallel between the Spirit in 3:8 and Jesus in 8:14 eliminates any need to identify the "we" and the "our" in 3:11 with the Johannine community.

John 3:18 mentions "the name of the unique Son of God," in which name people are to believe. The Son of God's uniqueness recalls the Prologue (1:14, 18, both times in connection with the Father). Since in the Prologue the unique one's name, in which people are to believe (1:12), is "the Word" (1:1 [*tris*], 14), identified there with "the light" that came into the world just as here in 3:19-21, presumably the name of the unique Son of God in which people are to believe at 3:18 is again "the Word." This is the name which God's unique Son *has* (genitive of possession), as opposed to the name which *is* "the unique Son of God" (genitive of apposition).[68]

---

see Jarl E. Fossum, *The Image of the Invisible God: Essays on the Influence of Jewish Mysticism on Early Christology* (NTOA 30; Göttingen: Vandenhoeck & Ruprecht, 1995), 109-33, esp. 125-26, and, more briefly, Henri Van den Bussche, *Le discours d'adieu de Jésus: Commentaires des chapitres 13 à 17 de l'évangile selon saint Jean* (Tournai: Casterman, 1959), 143.

66. 7:27-28b seems to indicate otherwise, but 7:28c-29 corrects the earlier statements by reducing them to Jesus' earthly origin.

67. Braun (*Jean le Théologien*, 3/1:120) notes the parallel between the testimony and the Word.

68. Cf. Phil 2:9-11, where "the name of Jesus" is not the name "Jesus," but is

That "the unique Son of God" is a descriptive phrase, not a name, is supported by several further considerations: (1) the insertion in attributive position of an adjective, "unique," into "the . . . Son of God"; (2) the absence of the phrase "of God" with "the unique Son" a couple of verses earlier in 3:16; (3) the absence of both "unique" and "of God" from "the Son" just one verse earlier in 3:17 and often elsewhere in John (see the concordance); and (4) the pairing and paralleling of "the Son of God" with other descriptive phrases as opposed to names: with "the one baptizing in the Holy Spirit" in 1:33-34, with "the King of Israel" in 1:49, and with "the Christ" in 11:27; 20:31. Because "the unique Son of God" in 3:18 appears to be a descriptive phrase for the owner of a name, then, and because the Prologue has established "the Word" as that owner's name, further references to Jesus' name should be taken likewise (14:13, 14, 26; 15:16, 21; 16:23, 24, 26; 20:31). The large number and wide distribution of these references display the pervasiveness of Word-Christology throughout John.

In contrast with Mark 2:19-20 par. Matt 9:15 and Luke 5:34-35, which portray Jesus as a bridegroom only by inference, John 3:29-34 portrays Jesus outright as a bridegroom, describes him as "the one coming from heaven," and gives him a "voice" with which he "testifies" to "what he has seen and heard" there and with which he "speaks the words of God" (τὰ ῥήματα τοῦ θεοῦ λαλεῖ). "Nobody receives his testimony," except that "the one receiving his testimony has certified that God is true." The passage reverberates with echoes of the Prologue and its portrayal of the Word, full of truth, who was in the beginning with God, came into

---

the name "Lord" which Jesus has and which every tongue will confess Jesus Christ to be. Against the notion that in John's Prologue "the light" has as much claim as "the Word" has to be considered the unique one's name, note that the unique one is never said to be the Word — he is simply called the Word, and this from the very start — whereas the Word is said to be the light, which has earlier been identified with the life that was "in" the Word. It is true that the fourth evangelist does not write concerning Jesus, "His name was the Word," as he writes concerning the Baptist, "His name was John" (1:6). But the evangelist does not have to, because he used "the Word" from the very start, and then referred back to that expression as "the name of him" (τὸ ὄνομα αὐτοῦ — N.B. the anaphoric definite article, as opposed to the anarthrous ὄνομα that introduces the name John), whereas the evangelist first called the Baptist "a man," so that it became natural, almost necessary, to write that his name was John.

the world, exegeted God, and was not received by his own, though he was received by some.[69] The statement that "he whom God has sent speaks the words (ῥήματα) of God" (3:34a) parallels the statement that "he [again Jesus, whom God has sent] gives the Spirit without measure" (3:34b, each statement being introduced with γάρ, "for").[70] That the "words" (ῥήματα) that Jesus speaks "are Spirit" (6:63) suits both the parallel in 3:34 between his speaking God's words and giving the Spirit without measure and his identification with the voice of the Spirit (see the foregoing discussion of 3:18).

To the woman of Samaria in 4:10 Jesus mentions "the gift of God" and pairs it in apparently synonymous parallelism with "the one speaking to you" (ὁ λέγων σοι) — this in connection with "living water" that "springs up into eternal life" (4:14). John 3:16 has already said, "God . . . gave his unique Son that everyone believing in him . . . might have eternal life." So Jesus himself is God's gift, and God's gift is a speaker. Since Jesus immediately quotes what he has spoken earlier ("Give me to drink"), we might think his self-identification as a speaker to be christologically insignificant: he identifies himself thus only to introduce the quotation. But later in his conversation with the Samaritan woman, 4:26 arouses second thoughts. There, in response to her statements, "I know that Messiah, the

69. Cf. Braun, *Jean le Théologien*, 3/1:103; Harris, *Prologue and Gospel*, 161. J. Jeremias ("νύμφη, νυμφίος," *TDNT* 4:1101) understands the voice of the bridegroom culturally: it is his joyous voice heard emanating from the nuptial chamber on discovering evidence of his bride's virginity. But to the contrary, see Mirjam and Ruben Zimmerman, "Der Freund des Bräutigams (Joh 3,29): Deflorations- oder Christuszeuge?" *ZNW* 90 (1999): 123-30. John understands the voice christologically.

70. For Jesus' giving the Spirit without measure to believers rather than God's doing so to Jesus, see 7:37-39; 20:22; 1 John 3:24; and Hans-Christian Kammler, "Jesus Christus und der Geistparaklet: Eine Studie zur johanneische Verhältnisbestimmung von Pneumatologie und Christologie," in Otfried Hofius and Hans-Christian Kammler, *Johannesstudien: Untersuchungen zur Theologie des vierten Evangeliums* (WUNT 88; Tübingen: Mohr-Siebeck, 1996), 170ff. Supporting Kammler is Hofius, "'Er gibt den Geist ohne Mass' Joh 3,34b," *ZNW* 90 (1999): 131-34; see also Felix Porsch, *Anwalt der Glaubenden: Das Wirken des Geistes nach dem Zeugnis des Johannesevangeliums* (Geist und Leben; Stuttgart: Katholisches Bibelwerk, 1978), 24-26.

one called Christ, is coming. When that one comes, he will announce (ἀναγγελεῖ) to us all things," Jesus says, "I am, the one speaking to you (ὁ λαλῶν σοι)." In view of the woman's reference to Messiah, i.e. Christ, it seems judicious to treat Jesus' response initially as elliptical and to fill it out: "I am Messiah, the one called Christ" (cf. 9:8-9). But the prominence of Jesus' divine "I am" elsewhere in John, most strikingly at 8:58 ("Before Abraham came into existence, I am"[71]), suggests a secondary such allusion here in 4:26.[72] Francis J. Moloney goes so far as to translate 4:26, "I AM [is] the one speaking to you."[73] "The one speaking to you" might also make some characteristically Johannine sense if taken as a predicate nominative without an ellipsis of "is" and in line with other Jesuanic statements strewn throughout John: "I am the one speaking to you" (cf. "I am the bread of life," "I am the light of the world," and so forth[74]).

Be those possibilities as they may, Jesus' response might well have stopped with "I am." But it does not. The added phrase, "the one speaking to you," harks back to 4:10 but is otiose here in 4:26 unless emphasis falls on Jesus as the speaker of a word, or as the Word who speaks. The probable allusion to Yahweh's statement in Isa 52:6 LXX, ἐγώ εἰμι αὐτὸς ὁ λαλῶν ("I myself am the one speaking") — a statement made in the immediate context of knowing Yahweh's "name" — supports an understand-

---

71. Margaret Davies (*Rhetoric and Reference in the Fourth Gospel* [JSNTSup 69; Sheffield: JSOT Press, 1992], 84-86) tries to evade the obvious by supposing an ellipsis in 8:58: "I am ['the light of the world,' as in 8:12]," so that "before Abraham" has to do with rank. But an ellipsis should not hark back so far as 8:12 is from 8:58, and πρίν means "before" in a temporal sense, not in the sense of rank.

72. For conflicting views see Gail R. O'Day, *Revelation in the Fourth Gospel: Narrative Mode and Theological Claim* (Philadelphia: Fortress, 1986), 72, and John Painter, *The Quest for the Messiah: The History, Literature, and Theology of the Johannine Community* (2d ed.; Nashville: Abingdon, 1993), 205; Andrea Link, *"Was redest du mit ihr?": Eine Studie zur Exegese-, Redaktions-, und Theologiegeschichte von Joh 4,1-42* (Biblische Untersuchungen 24; Regensburg: Pustet, 1992), 286-91; David Mark Ball, *"I Am" in John's Gospel: Literary Function, Background, and Theological Implications* (JSNTSup 124; Sheffield: Sheffield Academic Press, 1996), 60-67, 178-81.

73. Moloney, *Belief in the Word*, 154-56; idem, *The Gospel of John* (SP 4; Collegeville, Minn.: Liturgical Press, 1998), 130, 134.

74. John 6:35, 41, 48, 51; 8:12; 10:7, 9, 11, 14; 11:25; 14:6; 15:1, 5.

ing of John 4:10, 26 in terms of Jesus' name "the Word."[75] In 9:37 Jesus will likewise say to the man born blind but then healed, "You have seen him ['the Son of Man' — 9:35] and the one speaking with you (ὁ λαλῶν μετὰ σοῦ) is that one." Since 1:51 introduced the Son of Man as the angelic ladder of communication from an opened heaven to human beings on earth, it seems likely that Jesus' self-identification as the Son of Man and speaker in 9:37 also carries overtones of Word-Christology.

Back in 4:27 "his disciples came and were marveling that he was speaking (ἐλάλει) with a woman, yet no one said, 'What are you seeking?' or 'Why are you speaking (λαλεῖς) with her?'" She herself had asked, "How is it that you, being a Jew, ask to drink from me, being a woman, a Samaritan?" (4:9). But the Prologue has taught us that because Jesus is the Word, it is in his very nature to speak — even to a Samaritan woman, it turns out. She proceeds to report to her fellow townspeople, "Here! See a man who told me all that I ever did. Is this perhaps the Christ?" (4:29). As in 4:25-26, speech and Christhood appear in conjunction. And though "the word" (ὁ λόγος) in 4:37 refers to Jesus' saying, "One sows and another reaps," may there be a christological hint in the statement that "the word is true," especially in view of the description of the incarnate Word as "full . . . of truth" (1:14; cf. 4:42: "This is truly the Savior of the world"; 14:6: "I am . . . the truth"; and the many generally recognized instances of double entendre scattered throughout John)?

John 4:39 says that many Samaritans believed in Jesus "because of the word (τὸν λόγον) of the woman." What was the word that she "testified"? John quotes it again: "He told me all that I ever did." Her word reports his word. Then when he had stayed two days, many more believed because of their direct hearing of his word (διὰ τὸν λόγον αὐτοῦ — 4:41). "And they were saying to the woman, 'No longer do we believe because of your speech (διὰ τὴν σὴν λαλιάν), for we ourselves have heard

---

75. "Den unerhörten Anspruch, den Jesus zuvor durch sein Wort vertreten hat, begründet er durch sich selbst als den zu der Frau Redenden, durch — wie im Prolog angekündigt — seine Gegenwart im Logos" (Hinrichs, *"Ich Bin,"* 25). See also Birger Olsson, *Structure and Meaning in the Fourth Gospel: A Text-Linguistic Analysis of John 2:1-11 and 4:1-42* (ConBNT 6; Lund: Gleerup, 1974), 178-79.

and come to know that this one is truly the Savior of the world'" (4:42). Salvation by the word of Jesus the Word![76]

John 4:46-54 tells of Jesus' healing the son of a royal official. In Matt 8:5-13 and Luke 7:1-10 emphasis falls on the faith of a Gentile centurion as expressed in his plea, "But [Matthew: + 'only'] speak with a word . . . ," and as asterisked by Jesus' saying he had not found such great faith in Israel. In the comparable Matt 15:21-28 emphasis falls similarly on a Gentile woman's faith ("O woman, great is your faith"). The parallel Mark 7:24-30 emphasizes that same woman's "word" (τοῦτον τὸν λόγον). John 4:50, 53 puts the stress on *Jesus'* word: "The man believed the word (τῷ λόγῳ) which Jesus had spoken (εἶπεν) to him [cf. 2:22]. . . . Therefore the father knew that in the hour in which Jesus had said to him, 'Your sons lives,' ['the fever left him']; and he himself and his whole household believed." The royal official believed, but he did not ask Jesus to heal at a distance with a mere word, as in the Synoptics. John has Jesus the Word take the initiative to do so, against the request of the royal official that Jesus come down to Capernaum and perform a cure. And in contrast with Mark on the Syrophoenician woman, John does not underline any word of the royal official. The official had asked that Jesus "should heal his son (ἰάσηται αὐτοῦ τὸν υἱόν), for he was about to die" (4:47). But instead of hearing a word of healing, we hear a word of life: "Your son lives." What has the Prologue said about the Word? "In him was life" (1:4).[77]

Another of Jesus' signs follows immediately in 5:1-9. As in the first

---

76. Bultmann (*John*, 201) draws a contrast between the woman's λαλιάν as "mere words which in themselves do not contain that to which witness is borne" and Jesus' λόγον, "which refers to a statement of definite content." Has Bultmann forgotten that only two verses earlier John used λόγον for the woman's word? See further Schnackenburg, *John*, 1:456; Hinrichs, *"Ich Bin,"* 27-28.

77. The comparison between John and the Synoptics does not depend on John's use of them, but for such use see Ismo Dunderberg, "Johannine Anomalies and the Synoptics," in *New Readings in John: Literary and Theological Perspectives: Essays from the Scandinavian Conference on the Fourth Gospel, Aarhus 1997* (ed. Johannes Nissen and Sigfred Pedersen; JSNTSup 182; Sheffield: Sheffield Academic Press, 1999), 116-17.

two signs, Jesus performs this one by speaking a word, as opposed to putting the cripple in a pool when its water was troubled.[78] The subsequent discourse plays emphatically on Jesus' verbal method: "Amen, amen I say to you that the one hearing my word (τὸν λόγον μου) and believing the one who sent me has eternal life. . . . Amen, amen I say to you that an hour is coming, and now is, when the dead will hear the voice (τῆς φωνῆς) of the Son of God; and the ones who have heard will live" (5:24-25). If we think ahead to 14:1, where believing in Jesus parallels believing in God, the parallel in 5:24 between hearing Jesus' word and believing the one who sent him, viz., God, suggests that believing Jesus' word equates with believing in him himself. If the saying in Mark 9:37 par. Luke 9:48 ("and whoever accepts me accepts . . . the one who sent me") underlies John 5:24, it is notable that the Johannine version adds the element of Jesus' word for eternal life. And as Rudolf Schnackenburg has commented, Jesus' word is *verbum Verbi*, "the word of the Word."[79] The voice that makes this word audible and lifegiving sounds again in 5:28-29: "the hour is coming in which all who are in the tombs will hear his voice and come out." The voiced W/word is performative, as the case of Lazarus will demonstrate.

In 5:38 Jesus says to unbelievers in reference to God the Father, "And you do not have his word (λόγον) abiding in you, because he whom that one has sent — you do not believe this one." First to notice is the close association, almost a synonymous parallelism, between the Father's word and the one whom the Father has sent. Second, we know from the Prologue that Jesus is the Word who came into the world; from 6:56; 14:23; 15:4, 5 that Jesus abides in believers; and from 15:7 that Jesus' words (ῥήματα), which he got from the Father, abide in believers. And in 5:46-47 believing Jesus' words (ῥήμασιν) is the same as believing Jesus

---

78. Cf. Painter, *Quest,* 223.

79. Rudolf Schnackenburg, *The Gospel according to St John, Volume Two: Commentary on Chapters 5–12* (trans. Cecily Hastings, Francis McDonagh, David Smith, and Richard Foley; A Crossroad Book; New York: Seabury, 1980), 109. Cf. Painter, *Quest,* 233, and Bultmann, *John,* 252 ("the word of Jesus cannot be separated from his person"). Potterie (*La vérité,* 1:55n.40) agrees with Bultmann but rightly warns against him that Jesus' word is not he himself in the purely functional sense of revealing that he is the Revealer; rather, as himself the Word he reveals God.

himself, just as believing Moses is the same as believing the Mosaic text. Therefore it appears that in 5:38, to have the Father's word abiding in you equates with having Jesus the Word, whom the Father sent, abiding in you. Supporting this interpretation is Jesus' statement in 5:31, "I am testifying concerning myself." The follow-up, "my testimony is true," recalls again John's description of the incarnate Word as "full . . . of truth" (1:14).[80] And the references in 5:32-35 to the testimony of John the Baptist and to his being a lamplight recall his testifying in the Prologue concerning the Word as the true light.[81]

Jesus is "the bread of life" (6:35, 48, 51) in that he has "the words (ῥήματα) of eternal life" (6:68); and just as he is himself the bread of life that he gives, so also he is himself the words of life that he speaks. Since he is the bread, the bread that he gives is he himself, more particularly, his "flesh" (6:51, 53-55), i.e. the flesh that the Word became (1:14) so as to voice those words of eternal life. And since the Word was God (1:1, 18), the quotation of Isa 54:13 in John 6:45, "And they will all be taught by God" (διδακτοὶ θεοῦ — taking the genitive as subjective), implies being taught by Jesus as the Word who was God. Of course, the rest of 6:45 speaks of hearing and learning from alongside the Father.[82] But the next

---

80. Cf. Derek Tovey, *Narrative Art and Act in the Fourth Gospel* (JSNTSup 151; Sheffield: Sheffield Academic Press, 1997), 102, esp. n. 69, and Bultmann, *John,* 163: "the word of witness and that to which the word bears witness are identical."

81. First John 1:10 implies that God's word (λόγος) is in true believers: "If we say that we have not sinned, we make him [God] a liar and his word is not in us." The only word mentioned thus far in 1 John is "the Word of life," i.e. Jesus (1:1; cf. John 1:4); and according to 1 John 3:15, "eternal life," which acts as a christological title in 1:2; 5:20, abides in believers. So also 2:14: "the word (λόγος) of God abides in you." According to 1 John 2:4 and 2 John 2, the truth, which Jesus is according to John 14:6, abides in believers (cf. the abiding of God's seed and of the Father in believers according to 1 John 3:9, 24; 4:12-13, 15-16 with the statement in 2 John 9 that to have the Father is to have the Son, too).

82. Here and below I have awkwardly and literalistically translated παρά with "alongside," preceded by "from" when followed by the Greek genitive, to emphasize the allusion to the Word's preexistent presence with God the Father (cf. René Robert, "La double intention du mot final du prologue johannique," *Revue Thomiste* 87 [1987]: 439).

verse makes Jesus the one existing alongside God and the only one who has seen the Father, and this section closes with a reference to Jesus' teaching (6:59), so that to be taught by God means to be taught by Jesus the Word. Thus, coming to Jesus is the means as well as the result of hearing and learning from alongside the Father (6:45).

John 6:56 says it is the person that eats Jesus' flesh and drinks his blood who abides in him, and he in that person. But drinking Jesus' blood drops out in the immediately following vv. 57-59, so that Jesus' flesh captures the spotlight; for flesh is what the Word became (1:14). The reaction of many disciples follows naturally: "This word (λόγος) is hard. Who can hear it?" (6:60). As a saying of Jesus, this word is hard to hear, so that "his disciples grumble about *it*" (6:61). As Jesus himself, this Word is hard to hear, so that "many of his disciples backslid and were no longer walking around with *him*" (6:66). So hard this word/Word, in fact, that whether it is Jesus' saying or Jesus himself, no one can come to him unless it be given that person to do so (6:65; see also 6:44).[83]

But according to 6:63, "the flesh is profitable in no way." Why not, if the bread that Jesus gives for the life of the world is his flesh (6:51)? If being profitable in no way contrasts with making alive, as it does in 6:63, surely Jesus' flesh *is* profitable. He does not say, "*My* flesh is profitable in no way," however; rather, "*The* flesh is profitable in no way," just as in 3:6 "that which is born of the flesh" contrasts with "that which is born of the Spirit," and just as in 8:15 Jesus says that the Pharisees judge "according to the flesh." By contrast, his flesh is profitable, makes alive, because it is not ordinary flesh. It is the Word-made-flesh on whom the Spirit descended and abode (1:32). So he says, "The words (τὰ ῥήματα, synonymous with ὁ λόγος οὗτος in 6:60) that I have spoken (λελάληκα) to you are Spirit and are life," for "the Spirit is what makes alive" (6:63). The life-giving words that Jesus speaks are the Word-made-flesh that he is; for he not only *has* life in himself (1:4), he *is* the life (11:25; 14:6; cf. 1 John 1:1-2, where "the word [λόγου] of life," "the life" that "was manifested,"

---

83. On the ambiguity, or double meaning, of the word as Jesus' saying and as Jesus himself, see Bruce J. Malina and Richard L. Rohrbaugh, *Social-Science Commentary on the Gospel of John* (Minneapolis: Fortress, 1998), 137.

and "the eternal life that was with the Father and was manifested to us" function virtually as christological titles).[84]

Flesh as such profits in no way, then, so that apart from the Spirit the flesh of the Word would have done no good, but imbued with the Spirit did immense good.[85] For at the cross water as well as blood flowed out of Jesus' riven flesh. Water represents the Spirit as the agent of rebirth from above and the source of life (3:5; 7:37-39).[86] Put the equation of Jesus' words with *Spirit* and life (6:63) together with the statement that *Jesus* has the words of eternal life (6:68) and you get Jesus' identification with the Spirit, alongside a distinction from the Spirit, similar to the Word's identification with God, alongside a distinction from God, in the Prologue.[87]

The world's hating Jesus because of his testimony concerning it (7:7) recalls the statement in 1:11 that his own did not receive him as the Word. That is, the rejection of Jesus' testimony evinces his status and function as the rejected Word. In 7:11-17 his teaching replaces his testimony and contrasts with nobody's daring to speak about him openly for fear of the Jews. But despite the world's hatred and in contrast with the crowd's speaking about him only sub rosa, Jesus is loquacious — openly so, daringly so, as recognized by some Jerusalemites, "Look! He's speaking

---

84. On the equation of Jesus' words with Spirit, see Felix Porsch, *Pneuma und Wort* (Frankfurter Theologische Studien 16; Frankfurt: Knecht, 1974), 71-72, 195-204, 210-12; idem, *Anwalt der Glaubenden*, 120-31.

85. On the differences in John between flesh without the Spirit and flesh with the Spirit, see Marianne Meye Thompson, *The Incarnate Word: Perspectives on Jesus in the Fourth Gospel* (Peabody, Mass.: Hendrickson, 1988), 39-49. This book was originally titled *The Humanity of Jesus in the Fourth Gospel* (Philadelphia: Fortress, 1988).

86. Porsch, *Pneuma und Wort*, 53-81.

87. "The Spirit is christified; Christ is spiritualized" (C. F. D. Moule, *The Origin of Christology* [Cambridge: Cambridge University Press, 1977], 105). Cf. Jesus' "I am . . . the truth" (John 14:6) with "the Spirit is the truth" (1 John 5:7), and see George R. Beasley-Murray, *Gospel of Life: Theology in the Fourth Gospel* (Peabody, Mass.: Hendrickson, 1991), 98, and esp. Burge, *Anointed Community*, 83-84, 102: "the Spirit itself is identified with the Word. That is, the Spirit Jesus possesses and the Spirit he can offer are the words he speaks. Jesus as the Logos (the Word) becomes one with his message and presents himself in the words he offers."

openly" (7:26), and as later emphasized by the Word himself, "I have spoken openly to the world. I always taught in the synagogue and in the temple, where all the Jews come together; and in secret I spoke nothing" (18:20; see also 8:20: "he spoke these words in the treasury while teaching in the temple"). The Word is loud and clear: "Therefore Jesus shouted as he was teaching in the temple and saying, 'You both know me and you know where I am from'" (7:28). Notably, he himself is the subject matter of his didactic shout (see also 7:37-39; 12:44-50). And his teaching is marvelous: "therefore the Jews were marveling, saying, 'How does this [man] know letters though he has never learned [them]?'" (7:15). He knows them because his teaching and speech come from God, who sent him; hence, he is true just as the Word in the Prologue is true, and full of truth, because he was with the Father in the beginning and came into the world to exegete the Father.

The Jews ask, "What is this word (ὁ λόγος οὗτος) that he spoke (εἶπεν)?" It features Jesus himself: "You will seek me and not find me, and where I am you cannot come" (7:36), so that one could translate the preceding question, "*Who* (τίς) is this Word that he spoke?" Such a translation would not fit the Jews' point of view, of course; but it would fit John's point of view in that for him Jesus is himself the Word that he speaks. The word, "where I am you cannot come," reminds us that in the beginning, and before coming into the world, the Word was with God (1:1-2 with 9-11, 14). That the Jews do not comprehend this word ("What is this word?" they ask) reminds us that according to the Prologue the darkness did not comprehend the light that was the life of the Word (1:4-5). And the failure of the chief priests and the Pharisees to seize Jesus when he speaks about himself (7:32 with 44-46; see also 8:20 for Jesus' speaking "words" [ῥήματα] about himself as he was teaching in the temple) reminds us that according to the Prologue the darkness did not *ap*prehend the light which was the life of the Word any more than the darkness *com*prehended it (N.B. the double meaning of κατέλαβεν and Jesus' later volunteering himself to the band that came to seize him [cf. 11:57], so that instead of seizing him — i.e. apprehending him — they merely "took Jesus with [them]," συνέλαβον τὸν Ἰησοῦν [18:12; contrast the seizing of Jesus in Mark 14:44, 46 par. Matt 26:48, 50]).

After he cites himself as the source of living water (7:37-39), Jesus' listeners refer to "these words" (this time the plural of λόγος rather than of the synonymous ῥῆμα — 7:40) and split up into factions that confess him as "truly the prophet" and as "the Christ" and that deny his Christhood (7:40-43), just as in the Prologue some receive the λόγος and others do not. The current attempt to seize Jesus ends with the exclamation of chief priests' and Pharisees' officers, "A human being has never spoken like this!" (7:46). Of course not, because the Word who in Jesus became flesh was God![88] One is reminded that because of his rhetorical skill with words (λόγους), Protagoras was nicknamed "Word" (λόγος).[89]

Despite an earlier statement that if Jesus testifies concerning himself his testimony is not true, not admissible in a Jewish trial, he testifies extensively concerning himself in 8:12-20 and describes his testimony as true. It would be false of the Godman, who is full of truth and whose very name is "Word," not to testify concerning himself. So he makes himself the subject matter of his testimony just as he makes himself the subject matter of his words (cf. the use of ῥήματα, "words," in 8:20 to summarize Jesus' preceding self-testimony that he is "the light of the world," just as in the Prologue the Word is the light that comes into the world; also the parallel between ῥήματα and μαρτυρίαν, "testimony," in 3:32-34). It follows naturally that during his trial before Pilate, Jesus says, "I have been born for this purpose, and I have come into the world for this purpose, that I might testify to the truth [which is Jesus himself — 14:6]. Everyone who is of the truth hears my voice" (18:37). Jesus' voice testifies concerning himself as the truth embodied in the Word-made-flesh.

Back in 8:25 the Jews ask Jesus, "Who are you?" His answer, τὴν ἀρχὴν ὅ τι καὶ λαλῶ ὑμῖν, has caused commentators endless problems.

---

88. Cf. Donald A. Carson, *The Gospel according to John* (Leicester, England: Inter-Varsity Press, 1991), 331.

89. διὸ καὶ ἐπεκλήθη λόγος. So Hesychius in a scholium on Plato's *Republic* 600C as quoted by Suidas. For the text, see *Platonis Dialogi secundum Thrasylli Tetralogias* (ed. C. F. Hermann; 6 vols.; Leipzig: Teubner, 1892), 6:361; and for notices of this text, see Franz Passow, *Handwörterbuch der griechischen Sprache* (4 vols.; Leipzig: Fr. Chr. Wilh. Vogel, 1852), 2:78; LSJ s.v. λόγος IX 1. Cf. the use of λόγος in the plural for eloquence (Isocrates 3.1, 3; 9.11).

Even so skillful a commentator as Bultmann gives up trying to solve them.[90] Are Jesus' words a counter question or an exclamation rather than an answer? Should we treat ὅ τι as a conjunction (ὅτι, "that") rather than as a relative pronoun ("whatever")? Why the present tense of the verb when ἀρχήν, "beginning," belongs to the past? Are we dealing with an ellipsis, or with ellipses, and if so what should we supply? Most nettlesome of all, what use of the accusative does τὴν ἀρχήν represent? Standard commentaries survey the conflicting answers to these questions and provide pros and cons. I take the words of Jesus to be an answer, indeed a self-testimony in line with his immediately preceding self-testimony, not as a counter question. After all, the Jews have just asked about his identity. I take ὅ τι as a relative pronoun that introduces the meat of Jesus' answer to the question of his identity. And I take "I am," which has appeared three times in the verses leading up to the answer (see 8:23 [*bis*], 24), as implied in the answer. What then of τὴν ἀρχήν?

At this point we need to think in terms of John's text rather than in terms of what the historical Jesus said. For an analogy, take the Baptist's testimony to Jesus' preexistence (1:15, 30). Though Donald A. Carson defends the historicity of the Baptist's testimony that Jesus is God's lamb who takes away the sin of the world (1:29) — but defends it at the cost of saying that the Baptist did not understand the expiatory meaning of his own words — not even Carson mounts a defense of the historicity of the Baptist's testimony that Jesus preexisted.[91] Surely the testimony refers intratextually to the Word's preexistence according to the Prologue rather than to anything that the historical Baptist said. This sort of phenomenon is widely accepted as typical of John's Gospel.

Now the evangelist John uses the accusative of reference rather often,[92] and just two verses after the one in question there appears such an accusative: "They did not know that he was speaking to them in reference to the Father (τὸν πατέρα)" (8:27). The word order in Greek puts this ac-

90. Bultmann, *John,* 351-53.

91. Carson, *John,* 149-51.

92. Besides the two discussed in this paragraph, see 4:38 (ὅ), 52 (τὴν ὥραν); 6:10 (τὸν ἀριθμόν), 71 (τὸν Ἰούδαν); 8:54 (ὅν); 11:44 (τοὺς πόδας καὶ τὰς χεῖρας); 14:26 (πάντα); 21:21 (τί).

cusative at the head of its clause, just as τὴν ἀρχήν enjoys a forward position. If we take the accusative of reference in 8:27 as a cue for interpreting 8:25 and capitalize on the possibility of an intratextual reference in τὴν ἀρχήν, what emerges is an allusion to the Prologue: "In reference to the beginning [mentioned twice in 1:1-2]." Only at 8:25 does John put the definite article with ἀρχή. It is anaphoric; it harks back to the beginning in which the Word was. To be sure, ἀρχή has appeared in other connections between the Prologue and 8:25[93] and will reappear in other connections,[94] but only in the Prologue and 8:25 does ἀρχή appear in connection with Jesus' identity. The Prologue identifies Jesus as the Word, of course; and in 8:25 Jesus correspondingly identifies himself in terms of his speaking: "[I am] whatever I even speak to you." He is the Word being spoken by himself, rather as he testifies concerning himself.

Summarily, Jesus' statement, "In reference to the beginning [I am] whatever I even speak to you" (8:25), harks back to 8:24, "if you do not believe that I am." It connects the "I am" in 8:24 with the preexistence of the Word in the beginning according to 1:1. It prepares for Jesus' claim to preexistence in 8:58, "Before Abraham came into existence, I am." And it brings out Jesus' identity as the Word by calling attention to his speaking about himself. The following verses put further emphasis on his speech, which he got from the Father who sent him: "the things that I heard from alongside him ['the one who sent me'] — these things I speak (λαλῶ) in the world. . . . just as the Father taught me, I speak (λαλῶ) these things" (8:26-30, excerpts).[95]

93. See 2:11, "this beginning of the signs," and 6:64, "For Jesus knew from [the] beginning who they were that did not believe, and who it was that was going to betray him."

94. See 8:44; 15:27; 16:4.

95. On the whole question of 8:25, including textual criticism and arguments for and against the main views, see esp. Bruce M. Metzger, *A Textual Commentary on the Greek New Testament* (3d ed.; London: United Bible Societies, 1971), 223-24; R. W. Funk, "Papyrus Bodmer II (P⁶⁶) and John 8, 25," *HTR* 51 (1958): 95-100; E. R. Smothers, "Two Readings in Papyrus Bodmer II," *HTR* 51 (1958): 111-22; M. A. Pertini, "La genialidad grammatical de Jn 8, 25," *EstBib* 56 (1998): 371-408; Ed. L. Miller, "The Christology of John 8:25," *TZ* 36 (1980): 257-65. Miller, Thomas L. Brodie (*The Gospel according to John: A Literary and Theological Commen-*

In 8:31-38 Jesus addresses "the Jews who had believed him": "If you abide in my word (ἐν τῷ λόγῳ τῷ ἐμῷ), you are truly my disciples, and you will know the truth, and the truth will set you free" (vv. 31-32). The parallel between abiding in Jesus' word and abiding in Jesus (15:4-7) suggests that he himself is his word in which believers should abide to demonstrate the truth of their discipleship. John 15:2, 6, 8, too, deal with abiding in Jesus to demonstrate the truth of discipleship, so that the parallel between these two passages grows stronger.[96] Moreover, knowing the truth as a result of abiding in Jesus' word links with the incarnate Word, who is full of truth (1:14, 17) and is the truth (14:6). Right within 8:31-38, "the truth will set you free" (v. 32) parallels "if therefore the Son sets you free" (v. 36), so that Jesus the Son of God the Father (v. 38) is the truth revealed in Jesus' word, i.e. Jesus as the Word. Moreover again, "my word has no room in you" (ὁ λόγος ὁ ἐμὸς οὐ χωρεῖ ἐν ὑμῖν — v. 37) antithetically parallels Jesus' abiding in disciples (14:20, 23; 15:4, 5), just as Jesus' abiding in disciples is paralleled by the abiding of his words (ῥήματα) in them (15:7; cf. 15:3: "you are already clean on account of the word [τὸν λόγον] that I have spoken to you"). Once again an association between Jesus and his word, or words, is so close that we can legitimately think of an identification. When he speaks his word, or words, he speaks himself, not in the emphatic sense that he himself speaks, but in the sense that his identity as the Word provides the subject matter of his speech.

In 8:38 Jesus says, "The things that I have seen alongside the

---

tary [New York: Oxford University Press, 1993], 327), R. H. Lightfoot (*Saint John's Gospel: A Commentary* [ed. C. F. Evans; Oxford: Clarendon, 1956], 191), Ignace de la Potterie ("La notion de 'commencement' dans les écrits johanniques," in *Die Kirche des Anfangs* [ed. Rudolf Schnackenburg, Josef Ernst, and Joachim Wanke; ETS 38; Leipzig: St. Benno-Verlag, 1977], 386-89), and Henry Alford (*The Greek Testament: With a Critically Revised Text: A Digest of Various Readings: Marginal References to Verbal and Idiomatic Usage: Prolegomena: And a Critical and Exegetical Commentary* [4 vols., vol. 4 in two parts; 6th ed.; London: Rivingtons, 1868], 1:793) come close to the interpretation offered above, but none of them treat τὴν ἀρχήν as an accusative of reference.

96. Of course, John 15:9-10 speaks of abiding in Jesus' love, yet we do not say that he himself is love (though see 1 John 4:8: "God is love"). John does not name Jesus "Love," however, whereas he does name Jesus "Word."

[= 'my'] Father I am speaking (λαλῶ); and you, therefore, are doing the things that you have heard from alongside the [= 'your'] father [the Devil — 8:44[97]]." You would expect doing to be paired with seeing, and speaking to be paired with hearing (cf. 12:50 to a certain extent); but here it is vice versa so as to highlight Jesus' speaking. And what he speaks, i.e. the things he has seen alongside the Father, echoes the Word's being with God in the beginning (1:1-2).

John 8:39-47 offers a series of references to Jesus' speech. He says, "I have spoken to you the truth which I heard from alongside God" (v. 40). The last phrase reflects, as often in John, the Word's having been with God and having come into the world as the Word full of truth.[98] Just as Jesus is the truth, he is also the Word speaking it. He goes on to ask the Jews, "Why do you not understand my speech (τὴν λαλιάν)?" and answers his own question, "Because you are not able to hear my word (τὸν λόγον)" (v. 43). So the truth equates with Jesus' speech, which equates in turn with his word.[99] That he has heard the truth from alongside God does not forestall its equation with himself (to the contrary, see 14:6), so that as the truth he is the subject matter of what he heard from alongside God and has now spoken to humankind. Unlike those who cannot hear Jesus' word, "the one who is of God hears the words (τὰ ῥήματα) of God" (v. 47). So Jesus' speech and word, already equated with the truth which he himself is, equates also with the words of God. He is God's words as well as his own word, for as the Word he was God in the beginning.

Jesus' λόγος crops up again in 8:51-52: "Amen, amen I say to you, if anyone keeps my word, by no means will that person ever see death. . . . If

---

97. Nils Alstrup Dahl ("Der Erstgeborene Satans und der Vater des Teufels [Polyk. 7 1 und Joh 8 44]," in *Apophoreta* [BZNW 30; Berlin: Töpelmann, 1964], 70-85, esp. 76-79), and Günter Reim ("Joh. 8.44 — Gotteskinder/Teufelskinder. Wie antijudaistisch ist 'Die wohl antijudaistischste Äusserung des NT'?" *NTS* 30 [1984]: 619-24) conjecture a corruption in John's text, which originally made Cain the Jews' father.

98. See also John 6:46; 7:29; 8:26; 9:16, 33; 10:18; 15:15; 16:27; 17:7, 8; cf. 17:5 and Rev 2:28.

99. Barrett (*John,* 348) distinguishes between λαλιάν as audible speech and λόγον as a message. But see 4:41-42.

anyone keeps my word, by no means will that person ever taste death." These statements correspond to 5:24: "Amen, amen I say to you that the person hearing my word and believing the one who sent me . . . has transferred out of death into life." The correspondence indicates the synonymity of keeping Jesus' word, hearing it, and believing the Father who sent Jesus as the Word in whom is life (1:4; cf. 1 John 1:1: "what we have heard . . . concerning the Word of life").

John 8:51-52 may represent a development of the saying recorded in Mark 9:1: "Amen I say to you that there are certain people standing here who will by no means taste death until they see God's rule having come with power" (similarly the parallels in Matt 16:28 and Luke 9:27).[100] If it does, John's adding a double reference to the keeping of Jesus' word exhibits all the more an emphasis on Word-Christology. In 8:55 Jesus turns around to say that he keeps his Father's word (τὸν λόγον). But according to 14:23-24 the Father's word is Jesus' word, or words: "If anyone loves me, that person will keep my word (τὸν λόγον μου). . . . The person who does not love me does not keep my words (τοὺς λόγους μου), and the word (ὁ λόγος) that you hear is not mine but the Father's who sent me."

So in keeping the Father's word Jesus keeps the word that he passes on to his disciples, the word of life that negates death. Keeping that word means carrying out his function as the Word whom the Prologue describes as containing the light of life.[101] And it is in keeping Jesus' word to go wash in the Pool of Siloam that the man born blind receives sight so as to see the light of life (9:1-12). John translates Siloam as "Sent One" to call attention to Jesus as the Word whom God sent into the world from his preexistent location alongside God.

According to 10:19-21 the words of Jesus cause a division in his audience: "Again a division occurred among the Jews because of these words (τοὺς λόγους τούτους). And many of them were saying, 'He has a demon and is raving. Why do you hear him?' Others were saying, 'These are not

---

100. See Barnabas Lindars, "Discourse and Tradition: The Use of the Sayings of Jesus in the Discourses of the Fourth Gospel," *JSNT* 13 (1981): 95-96.

101. Against Harnack, "Ueber das Verhältnis," 207.

the words (ταῦτα τὰ ῥήματα) of a demoniac. A demon cannot open a blind man's eyes, can it?'" By now John's audience know that "these words" are the words of the Word who was with God and was God, quite the opposite of a demon-possessed man. Verses 1-18 contain the words referred to. In them Jesus says he is the good shepherd who calls (φωνεῖ) his own sheep by name, whose voice (φωνή) his sheep hear and recognize, and who has other sheep that will hear his voice. And Jesus says he is the door of the sheep for their entrance into salvation and life, the good shepherd who at his Father's command lays down his life for the sheep, and the one who knows God as his Father and is known by God. In other words, Jesus is again the subject matter of his words.

Dialogue with the Jews continues in 10:34-36: "Jesus answered them, 'Is it not written in your law, "I said, 'You are gods'" [Ps 82:6]? If he called (εἶπεν) those ones "gods" to whom the word of God became (ὁ λόγος τοῦ θεοῦ ἐγένετο) — and the Scripture cannot be broken — are you saying in reference to him whom the Father sanctified and sent into the world, "You are blaspheming," because I said, "I am God's Son"?'" Who were the ones to whom the word of God "became"? Several answers have been offered: the nation of Israel, Israel's judges, individuals who ascended to heaven, and angels.[102] What was the word of God that "became" to them? The law, or heavenly revelations, or the preexistent Logos.[103] When did the word of God "become" to them? In the OT period. And what is the nature of Jesus' argument? Most commentators answer that the argument is *a fortiori:* if God called those ones "gods" to whom the word of God became, how much more appropriate it is for him whom the Father

---

102. See M. J. J. Menken, "The Use of the Septuagint in Three Quotations in John: Jn 10,34; 12,38; 19,24," in *The Scriptures in the Gospels* (ed. C. M. Tuckett; BETL 131; Leuven: Leuven University Press, 1997), 370-82; Jerome H. Neyrey, "'I Said: You Are Gods': Psalm 82:6 and John 10," *JBL* 108 (1989): 647-63.

103. For the preexistent Logos, see Anthony Tyrrell Hanson, "John's Citation of Psalm LXXXII," *NTS* 11 (1964-65): 158-62; idem, "John's Citation of Psalm LXXXII Reconsidered," *NTS* 13 (1966-67): 363-67; idem, *Prophetic Gospel,* 144-49; Martin Hengel, "Die Schriftauslegung des 4. Evangeliums auf dem Hintergrund der urchristlichen Exegese," *Jahrbuch für Biblische Theologie* 4 (1989): 260-63 (with references to earlier literature).

sanctified and sent into the world to call himself God's Son. Herman N. Ridderbos argues, however, that no *a fortiori* is needed; the argument consists only in the point that if certain ones were called gods in the OT, then Jesus is not blaspheming by calling himself God's Son.[104] A few commentators toy with the possibility of an allusion to Jesus as the Word of God, but decide that since Jesus did not come on the scene in the OT period such an allusion could at most constitute a secondary meaning.[105]

Now in John 10:36 the aorist verbs ἡγίασεν ("sanctified") and ἀπέστειλεν ("sent") refer without question to Jesus' earthly ministry (cf. his use in the Synoptics of the aorist ἦλθον, "I came," for that ministry[106]). We have good reason, then, to take the aorist verb ἐγένετο

104. Herman N. Ridderbos, *The Gospel according to John: A Theological Commentary* (trans. John Vriend; Grand Rapids, Mich.: Eerdmans, 1997), 374-75. See also Richard Jungkuntz, "An Approach to the Exegesis of John 10:34-36," *CTM* 35 (1964): 556-58.

105. See Joong Suk Suh, *The Glory in the Gospel: Restoration of Forfeited Prestige* (Oxford, Ohio: M. P. Publications, 1995), 117-21; M. E. Boismard, "Jésus, le Prophète par excellence, d'après Jean 10, 24-39," in *Neues Testament und Kirche* (ed. Joachim Gnilka; Freiburg: Herder, 1974), 171; Raymond E. Brown, *The Gospel according to John: Introduction, Translation, and Notes* (2 vols.; AB 29-29A; Garden City, N.Y.: Doubleday, 1970), 1:809-10; Bruce G. Schuchard, *Scripture within Scripture: The Interrelationship of Form and Function in the Explicit Old Testament Citations in the Gospel of John* (SBLDS 133; Atlanta: Scholars Press, 1992), 59-70; Andreas Obermann, *Die christologische Erfüllung der Schrift im Johannesevangelium: Eine Untersuchung zur johanneischen Hermeneutik anhand der Schriftzitate* (WUNT 2/83; Tübingen: Mohr-Siebeck, 1996), 178-85, 380-87; and Hanson's discussions, cited above. Though Jesus *bore* the preexistent Logos, Hanson does not think that Jesus *was* the preexistent Logos that came to Israel at Sinai. Perhaps it should be said here that despite Moses' writing about Jesus (1:45; 5:45-46), 1:17 draws enough of a contrast between the giving of the law through Moses and the coming of grace and truth through Jesus Christ to forestall a unification of these events through a double reference in 10:34-35. The denials in 1:18 that anyone has ever seen God and in 6:32 that Moses gave the bread from heaven undermine further such a double reference, as they do also a correlation in 10:34-35 between Jesus as the Word of God and Jesus as a prophet like Moses (Deut 18:15). Jesus as the Word of the Prologue makes better Johannine sense. See the following discussion.

106. See Eduardo Arens, *The HΛΘON-Sayings in the Synoptic Tradition: A Historical-Critical Investigation* (OBO 10; Göttingen: Vandenhoeck & Ruprecht, 1976).

("became") as having the same referent, just as this very same verb did in 1:14, "and the Word became (ἐγένετο) flesh and tabernacled among us," and 1:17, "Grace and truth became (ἐγένετο) through Jesus Christ." "The Word of God" in 10:35 is thus a direct and exclusive reference to Jesus as God's Word; and the ones "to whom the Word of God became" are Jesus' contemporaries, much as in 10:10 he said, "I came [ἦλθον] that they ['the sheep'] might have life," and as in 1:11 "he came [ἦλθεν] to his own, and his own did not receive him." For John's synonymous use of ἐγένετο and ἦλθεν see 1:6-7. The use in 10:35 of ἐγένετο instead of ἦλθεν is due to the OT formula ויהי דבר יהוה אל, "the word of Yahweh became to," which in the LXX comes out as καὶ ἐγένετο/ἐγενήθη λόγος/ ῥῆμα κυρίου πρός (cf. Luke 3:2: ἐγένετο ῥῆμα θεοῦ ἐπὶ Ἰωάννην). M. J. J. Menken notes that in John 10:35 "the word of God" replaces "the word of the Lord" in the OT formula, because John uses κύριος usually for Jesus and for God only in 12:13, 38 in dependence on the OT.[107] We might add that the Prologue's association and identification of the Word with God contribute to the replacement.

All in all, then, Jesus treats Ps 82:6, not as a historical statement about anybody in OT times, but as a predictive prophecy fulfilled by his coming to his contemporaries, called "gods" by that text because Jesus has appeared on the scene to them, and has done so as the Word of God. The fulfillment demonstrates the unbreakability of Scripture and falsifies the charge of blasphemy. The law can in fact be broken by disobedience. According to 7:23, failure to perform circumcision on the Sabbath (if the Sabbath falls on the eighth day after birth, it is understood) would count as a breaking of "the law of Moses," just as 5:18 speaks of breaking the Sabbath. The verb for breaking (λύω) is the same as that used in 10:35. Similarly in Matt 5:19 this verb occurs for breaking "one of these least commandments" of "the law." Moreover, the compound form of the verb (καταλύω) stands in Matt 5:17-18 as an antonym to πληρόω, "fulfill," and in parallel with γίνομαι, "come to pass," which in turn contrasts with παρέρχομαι, "pass away." Therefore in John 10:34-36 the unbreakability

---

107. Menken, "Use of the Septuagint," 372. See the concordance for John's many uses of κύριος for Jesus.

of Scripture fits a scheme of prediction and fulfillment better than it fits a historical reference. Jesus' statements in 5:39, "You search the Scriptures . . . and those are the ones testifying concerning me," and 46, "For that one [Moses] wrote concerning me," have prepared John's audience to understand the OT quotation and its interpretation at 10:35-36 in terms of Word-Christology.[108] And numerous further passages will confirm this understanding: 12:37-41 ("in order that the word of Isaiah the prophet might be fulfilled . . . . These things Isaiah said because he saw his [Jesus'] glory [defined in 1:14 as the glory of the incarnate Word] and spoke about him" [cf. 12:34: "We have heard from the law that the Christ abides forever"]); 13:18 ("but in order that the Scripture might be fulfilled . . ."); 15:25 ("But in order that the word written in their law might be fulfilled . . ."); 19:24 ("in order that the Scripture might be fulfilled, which says . . ."), 36-37 ("For these things happened in order that the Scripture might be fulfilled . . . . And again another Scripture says . . ."); 20:9 ("For they did not yet know the Scripture that it is necessary for him to rise from the dead"). Three or four of these passages cite the Psalms, as does 10:34. Since in the Prologue the Word not only was with God and came from God but also was God, we could even think that in 10:35-36 "the Word of God" means both the Word spoken by God (τοῦ θεοῦ as a subjective genitive) and the Word who was God (τοῦ θεοῦ as a genitive of apposition).

It might be objected against the foregoing interpretation that if it were correct, Jesus would be quoted as saying, "If he called you [not 'those ones'] gods . . . ." But the expression "those ones" includes more people than Jesus' immediate audience, who have just taken up stones with which to stone him (10:31-33); for, again in reference to 1:11, "he came

---

108. On the need to take account of a prophetically predictive implication in the statement, "The scripture cannot be broken," see Hanson, "John's Citation of Psalm LXXXII," 161; idem, *Prophetic Gospel,* 145-46, in dependence on Jungkuntz, "An Approach to the Exegesis of John 10.34-36," 556-65. In private conversation Moisés Silva suggested to me that Jesus' calling the Scripture "your law" evoked a reference to its unbreakability, but Silva admitted that law-breaking as a violation of the law would make no sense in this passage. The aorists εἶπα, "I said," and εἶπεν, "he said [in the sense of 'called']," refer of course to God's speaking in the past what is recorded in Ps 82:6.

to his own, and his own did not receive him." His immediate audience falls short of making up the entirety of "his own," and as recently as 9:39-41 he has used the third person plural alongside the second person plural in reference to his audience. Therefore the objection would fail.

It might also be objected that nowhere in John does Jesus say outright, "I am the Word of God," as he does say outright, "I am God's Son" (10:36). But nowhere in John or the Synoptics does Jesus say, "I am the Son of Man," yet everybody understands that at least the textual Jesus (if not the historical Jesus) uses that phrase for himself some of the time (if not all the time — for instances in John, see 1:51; 3:13, 14; 5:27; 6:27, 53, 62; 8:28; 9:35; 12:23, 34 [*bis*]; 13:31). So this objection, too, would fail to disprove that Jesus was the Word of God that came to those whom the law called gods, i.e. Jesus' contemporaries.

Commentators often note that after the Prologue "the Word" does not appear absolutely in John. Therefore it might be objected once again that in 10:35 the addition of the phrase "of God" to "the word" prohibits an equation of "the word of God" there with "the Word" in the Prologue.[109] But the phrase "in the beginning" made it inappropriate in the Prologue that "of God" should be added; for "the word of God" connotes a message, and in the beginning there was no one to whom a message could be addressed. Once all things have come into existence through the Word (1:3), however, and after the Word has entered the world by being made flesh (1:14), "the Word of God" becomes a meaningful designation of Jesus as God's message to humankind. Hence, the absoluteness of "the Word" in John's Prologue puts no roadblock in the way of taking "the Word of God" in 10:35 as a designation of Jesus, just as that very phrase indubitably designates him in Rev 19:13 (cf. "the Word of life" — nonabsolute — in 1 John 1:1).

Already in the Prologue, moreover, the equation of the Word with God makes the Word prospectively God's Word in effect though not in phraseology, as does also the Word's being the unique one who "exegeted" God (1:1, 18). Those who think that John presents Jesus as Wisdom incar-

109. Cf. Georg Strecker, *Theology of the New Testament* (ed. Friedrich Wilhelm Horn; trans. M. Eugene Boring; New York: Walter de Gruyter, 2000), 473.

nate despite failing ever to use the word "wisdom," much less to identify Jesus as Wisdom, should have no trouble accepting that the Word who was *with* God, and *was* God, is the Word *of* God (cf. Ign. *Magn.* 8:2). If Jesus appears as the Word of God in John 10:35, we should dismiss the oft-repeated statement that after the Prologue λόγος ceases to apply to Jesus.[110]

According to 11:28-29 Mary heard that Jesus the teacher was calling her. The verb for calling, φωνεῖ, refers to Jesus' voice. As one of his sheep, Mary recognized that voice as her shepherd's (even though it was relayed to her by Martha). Mary got up quickly and started going to him. On arrival at the tomb of her brother Lazarus, Jesus said to his Father, "I spoke on account of the crowd standing around, in order that they may believe that you sent me" (11:42). Jesus' speaking aims to elicit people's believing, just as according to John's Prologue the Word came into the world to elicit people's believing in his name (1:9-12). Then Jesus "shouted with a loud voice (φωνῇ μεγάλῃ ἐκραύγασεν), 'Lazarus, come out!'" In 12:17 a back-reference to this shout underlines Jesus' voice: "he called (ἐφώνησεν) Lazarus." As usual, Jesus' word was performative, for Lazarus came out of the tomb, as to be expected from 5:25: "Amen, amen I say to you that an hour is coming, and now is, when the dead will hear the voice of the Son of God, and the ones having heard will live" (cf. Ezek 37:1-14, where Yahweh's word brings life to the dead). The verb for Jesus' shouting, κραυγάζω, occurs only nine times in the NT, six of them in John. It emphasizes the loudness of Jesus' voice, and that loudness stresses the power and authority of his word, his power and authority as the Word of God (cf. Rev 1:10). Through Jesus' speaking on account of the crowd standing around and through his shouting with a loud voice so as to raise Lazarus from the dead, Martha saw "the glory of God" (11:40) in accordance with the beholding of the glory of the incarnate Word, glory as of the unique one from alongside the Father (1:14).

In John 12:27 Jesus asks, "And what should I say (εἴπω)?" and in 12:36 he declares, "These things I have spoken (ἐλάλησεν)." His inter-

---

110. For an especially clear example of such a statement, see H. J. Holtzmann, *Evangelium, Briefe und Offenbarung des Johannes* (2d ed.; HKNT 4; Freiburg im Breisgau: Mohr-Siebeck, 1893), 8-9.

vening words, then, are framed by formal references to his speaking. The next section containing Jesus' words is likewise framed by such references: "But Jesus shouted and said (ἔκραξεν καὶ εἶπεν)" (12:44); "In reference to the things that I speak (λαλῶ), according as the Father has spoken (εἴρηκεν) to me, thus I speak (λαλῶ)" (12:50). So Jesus' loud voice corresponds to the Father's thunder-like voice in intervening verses (12:28-29) — naturally, since Jesus is the Word *of God* (10:35-36).

In 12:47-48 Jesus says he is not judging the person who hears his words (ῥημάτων) but does not keep them; rather, the word (ὁ λόγος) which he has spoken (ἐλάλησα) will "at the last day" judge the person who fails to receive his words (ῥήματα), which failure equates with rejecting him (12:48) and with failure to receive Jesus the Word (1:11). The demonstrative pronoun ἐκεῖνος refers back to, and lays emphasis on, "the word which I have spoken." Earlier, Jesus said the Father "has given all judgment to the Son" (5:22; see also 5:27, 30; 8:16), so that — although Jesus presently judges no one (see also 8:15), because he came not to judge the world but to save the world (12:47; see also 3:17) — he will be the self-spoken Word that judges unbelievers at the last day (see also Rev 19:11-16 for Jesus as "the Word of God" coming in judgment).

Jesus is his Father's word as well as his own, as he himself said, "I did not speak (ἐλάλησα) from myself; rather, the Father who sent me — he has given me a commandment in reference to what I should say (εἴπω) and what I should speak (λαλήσω). And I know that his commandment is eternal life. Therefore in reference to the things that I speak, according as the Father has spoken to me, thus I speak" (12:49-50). Since life is in the Word (1:4) and Jesus is "the life" (11:25; 14:6), "the Word of life" (1 John 1:1), and "life eternal" (1 John 5:20), the statement that the Father's commandment is eternal life implies that Jesus is that commandment in the same sense that he is the words that make up the Word.[111]

---

111. Carson (*John,* 453) comments aptly, "Jesus' speech is a reflection of his person. Not only is what Jesus says just what the Father has told him to say, but he himself is the Word of God, God's self-expression (1:1)." See also Robert Kysar, *John* (ACNT; Minneapolis: Augsburg, 1986), 204 ("chapters 1–12 end . . . much as they started — with the claim that Jesus is the Word of God"), and Harris, *Prologue and Gospel,* 164 ("his [Jesus'] present speech is identical with the speech of God, and ex-

Mark 8:38 (par. Matt 16:27 and Luke 9:26) records Jesus' saying, "For whoever is ashamed of me and my words (τοὺς ἐμοὺς λόγους) in this adulterous and sinful generation, the Son of Man will also be ashamed of him whenever he comes in the glory of his Father with the holy angels." If John has developed Jesus' statements in John 12:47-50 out of that synoptic saying, we can see an expansion of the earlier reference to Jesus' words. ῥήματα has replaced λόγους, and the plural λόγους has changed to the singular λόγος. Being ashamed of Jesus' words has changed to rejecting him and not receiving his words, for his identity lies in his words. And in line with Word-Christology, Jesus' speaking what the Father commanded him enlarges the verbal element.

In 13:13-14 Jesus commends the disciples' calling him "Teacher" (ὁ διδάσκαλος), affirms that he is in fact their teacher, and then calls himself "Teacher" (cf. 20:16, where Mary Magdalene calls Jesus "Rabbouni," which John takes care to translate as "Teacher" and notes that she recognized Jesus by hearing him call her by name, as in 10:1-5, 16, 27 the good shepherd calls his sheep by name and they recognize his voice). Not surprisingly, then, Jesus goes on to speak continually of his word, words (the plural of both λόγος and ῥῆμα), commandment, and commandments, and of his speaking qua speaking (13:34; 14:15, 21, 23-26, 28-30; 15:3, 7, 10, 12, 17, 20). As to Jesus' "new commandment, that you love one another, according as I loved you that you also love one another" (13:34), it builds on the OT commandment that the synoptic Jesus quoted, "You shall love your neighbor as [you love] yourself" (Mark 12:31, 33; Matt 5:43; 19:19; 22:39; Luke 10:27). Later we will explore the differences between these commandments. For now it suffices to note that as the Word who is God, Jesus gives as his own a commandment that replaces God's commandment in the Mosaic law.[112]

---

actly reproduces what his Father has commanded him to say"). Contrast Harnack, "Ueber das Verhältnis," 206-8. Harnack thinks so diachronically in terms of sources that he underestimates the interrelatedness of John's Prologue with the rest of the Fourth Gospel.

112. The switching from λόγον to λόγους and back to λόγος undermines the statement of Barrett (*John*, 505), "It is shown at 14.23f. that a distinction should be drawn between *word* (singular) and *words* (plural). The former means the divine mes-

Jesus asks, "Do you not believe that I [am] in the Father and the Father is in me? The words (ῥήματα) that I say (λέγω) to you I do not speak (λαλῶ) from myself; but the Father, abiding in me, does his works. Believe me, that I [am] in the Father and the Father [is] in me. But if not, believe because of the works themselves" (14:10-11). As in the Prologue the Word was with God, in the Father's bosom, so here Jesus' words arise out of the mutual indwelling of him and the Father. Also, the conjoining of Jesus' words and the Father's works highlights the performative power of the words. Just as the works are visible words, then, the words are audible works. And so much is Jesus the Word that even after his going back to the Father, the Holy Spirit will teach the disciples all things and remind them of all that Jesus told them (14:26). Thus in the interests of Word-Christology, the Holy Spirit's teaching the disciples what *they* should say, according to the Synoptics (Mark 13:11 par. Matt 10:19-20 and Luke 12:11-12), is exchanged in John for the Holy Spirit's reminding them of what *Jesus* said. Not only what Jesus said in the past, but also what as the glorified Word he will yet say: "the Spirit of truth will guide you into all the truth, for he will not speak from himself, but he will speak *as many things as he will hear* and will announce to you the coming things. . . . he will *take [them] from me* and announce [them] to you" (John 16:13-15).[113]

According to 15:3 the disciples are clean because of the word (λόγον) that Jesus has spoken to them. According to 13:5, 10 they are clean because they have been washed with water; and 1 John 1:7, 9 speak of Jesus' blood as cleansing believers from all sin. Our minds turn naturally to John 19:34: "with his spear one of the soldiers pierced his [Jesus'] side, and immediately there came out blood and water." So the word be-

---

sage brought by Jesus taken as a whole, the latter is nearer in meaning to ἐντολαί, precepts." Barnabas Lindars (*The Gospel of John* [NCB; London: Oliphants, 1972], 477) comes closer to the mark in writing that the plural ἐντολαί "refers to the manifold applications of the one commandment to love one another (compare 15.10 and 12)."

113. Cf. Käsemann, *Testament of Jesus*, 46: "John . . . identified the Spirit with the voice of Jesus which in the form of the Paraclete [on earth] continues to speak from heaven to the disciples when he himself [Jesus] is no longer with them"; see also Potterie, *La vérité*, 2:362-63.

cause of which the disciples are clean lines up with the cleansing blood and water of the Word-made-flesh (1:14).

The abiding of Jesus' words (ῥήματα) in the disciples (15:7) parallels the abiding of Jesus himself in them (15:4, 5), because as the Word he is his words.[114] "The word" (τοῦ λόγου) that Jesus "has spoken" to the disciples and that they are to "remember" is a word about his lordship over them: "A slave is not greater than his master [= 13:16]. If they have persecuted me, they will persecute you, too. If they have kept my word (λόγον), they will keep yours, too" (15:20, the last statement being ironic, of course). We have already seen that keeping Jesus' word means hearing it, i.e. hearing him as the Word, and believing the one who sent him (5:24; 8:51). It looks as though the saying in 15:20 grew out of the one recorded in Matt 10:24-25: "A disciple is not above the teacher, neither a slave above his master. [It is] sufficient for the disciple that he become as his teacher and [that] the slave [become] as his master." If the Johannine saying did grow out of the Matthean one, John's addition of Jesus' word is notable. Again that word is paired with Jesus' works so as to make his speech visible and his works audible: "If I had not come and spoken (ἐλάλησα) to them, they would not have had sin. . . . If I had not done the works among them that no one else had done, they would not have had sin" (15:22, 24). And in 15:25 "the word" (ὁ λόγος) written in the Jews' law and hated by them ("They hated me without a cause" — Pss 35:19; 69:5) is Jesus, written in the law as the "me" who is hated by his unbelieving contemporaries (cf. John 1:45; 2:17; 10:34-35; 12:14, 16).

John 16:1 starts with a warning that the disciples should not be "scandalized," i.e. "led to apostatize": "These things I have spoken (λελάληκα) to you that you should not be led to apostatize" (cf. Mark 13:22). The text could have read only, "You should not be led to apostatize," much as in Mark 13:5 (par. Matt 24:4 and Luke 21:8): "Beware lest anyone lead you astray." But no, the emphasis in John falls on Jesus' speaking; and there follows a cornucopia of references to his speaking:

---

114. See Brown, *John*, 2:662: "Jesus and his revelation are virtually interchangeable, for he is incarnate revelation."

"But these things I have spoken to you . . . I told you. But these things I did not tell you from the beginning . . . . I have spoken these things to you . . . . however, I am telling you the truth . . . . I have yet many things to tell you . . . . What is this that he is saying to us? . . . What is this that he is saying? . . . what he speaks. . . . I said . . . . Amen, amen I say to you . . . . Amen, amen I say to you . . . . I have spoken these things to you in figures. An hour is coming when I will no longer speak to you in figures; rather, I will report (ἀπαγγελῶ) plainly to you concerning the Father. . . . Behold, now you are speaking plainly, and you are not saying anything figurative. . . . These things I have spoken to you . . . . Jesus spoke these things" (16:4, 6, 7, 12, 17, 18, 19, 20, 23, 25, 29, 33; 17:1). Where in the Synoptics do we find anything even approaching such a magnification of Jesus' words? Surely this magnification develops out of John's portrayal of Jesus as the Word.

In prayer Jesus tells his Father that the disciples have kept the Father's word (λόγον — 17:6). This keeping of the Father's word amounts to hearing Jesus as the Word (see 5:24; 8:51 with the foregoing comments). "All things whatever that the Father has given [to Jesus]" (17:7) equate with "the words" (τὰ ῥήματα) that the Father has given him and that the disciples have received (17:8). The disciples have received these words in that they have come to know truly that Jesus came forth from the Father and in that they have believed the Father sent him (17:8 again).

Jesus says, "I am speaking (λαλῶ) these things in the world" (17:13) and "I have given them your word (λόγον)" (17:14). The latter statement parallels the one in 17:8 that Jesus has given the disciples the words that the Father has given him. Since these words in 17:8 equate with the word that in 17:14 is not from the world, in giving believers the Father's word Jesus gave himself as the Word that is not from the world. Jesus' having come forth from the Father and the disciples' having received Jesus' words echo similar statements in the Prologue concerning the Word. Thus "your [the Father's] word" (ὁ λόγος ὁ σός) in which according to 17:17 believers are sanctified, and which is truth, is Jesus himself, who earlier called himself the truth, whom the Prologue described as "the true light" and as "full of . . . truth," and who says here that he is sanctifying himself on be-

43

half of believers (1:1-18; 11:25; 14:6; 17:17, 19).[115] The ἐν before τῇ ἀληθείᾳ might be taken as instrumental ("*by* the truth"), but a christological reference favors a locative ἐν, "in the truth," so as to link sanctification in the word with abiding in Christ (15:1ff.). Believers, then, are sanctified in the Father's word because they abide in the self-sanctified Christ, who is that Word.[116]

The statement that the Father's word is truth seems to quote Ps 119:142: "And your law is truth." But the substitution of λόγος for the law reflects the Word-Christology of John (cf. the multiple interchanges of "word" and "truth" in 8:31-55, and 1 John 1:8, 10: "If we were to say that we have no sin, . . . the truth is not in us. . . . If we were to say that we have not sinned, . . . his word [λόγος, previously described as having been with the Father and manifested to us — 1:1-2] is not in us"). We may then at least ask whether in John 17:20 "their word" (τοῦ λόγου αὐτῶν) might allude to Jesus himself insofar as God has given Jesus as his word to the disciples and in that Jesus has given himself as God's word to them, so that he is now their word, too, the subject matter of their word on account of which others will believe in Jesus.[117]

In the account of Jesus' arrest he takes the initiative by saying, "Whom do you seek?" (18:4, 7). It is his *saying*, "I am," that causes the arresting band to go backward and fall to the ground (18:5-6). And it is his *word*, "If then you seek me, let these go," that allows the band to arrest

115. Cf. Nigel Turner, *Grammatical Insights into the New Testament* (Edinburgh: T. & T. Clark, 1965), 8-11; Merrill C. Tenney, "The Gospel of John," in *Expositor's Bible Commentary* (12 vols.; Regency Reference Library; Grand Rapids, Mich.: Zondervan, 1981), 9:165; Obermann, *Die christologische Erfüllung,* 381-82; Van den Bussche, *Le discours d'adieu de Jésus,* 149; and against Gordon H. Clark (*The Johannine Logos* [Nutley, N.J.: Presbyterian and Reformed, 1972], 55), who takes "your word" as "the Scripture."

116. Cf. 15:3, and see the foregoing comments on 10:34-35 against drawing a sharp distinction between the absolute and nonabsolute uses of λόγος in John.

117. Cf. Heinrich Schlier, *Das Ende der Zeit: Exegetische Aufsätze und Vorträge III* (Freiburg: Herder, 1971), 18: "Der Geist, aber auch die Jünger sind Zeugen Jesu. Natürlich nicht nebeneinander, sondern so, dass sie durch ihn und er durch sie Jesus in seiner Wahrheit verkünden. In deiser Weise setzt der Jünger Wort das Wort Jesu, und das ist Gottes Wort, fort, vgl. 15,20; 17,20."

him and effects the salvation of his disciples (18:8). There results a fulfillment of Jesus' earlier "word that he spoke" (ὁ λόγος ὃν εἶπεν): "In reference to those whom you [the Father] have given me, I lost not even one of
them" (18:9; cf. 6:39). Is Jesus himself this spoken word as well as the
speaker of it? Probably yes, because he is the doer of the action (not losing
one of those that the Father has given him) of which he spoke. See also
18:32 with 3:14; 8:28; and especially 12:32-33 for the fulfillment of another word (λόγος) of Jesus in which he plays the central role.

In Mark 14:60-62 par. Matt 26:62-64 Jesus does not answer the testimony given against him before the Sanhedrin, though he does answer
the high priest's question whether he is the Christ, the Son of the Blessed
One. Luke 22:66-70 keeps Jesus' answer to the high priest's question
about his identity but drops the antagonistic testimony and therefore Jesus' nonanswer to it. John 18:19 likewise drops that testimony and Jesus'
nonanswer, but reserves till later the question about his identity and
changes the high priest's question into one about Jesus' disciples (literally,
"learners") and "teaching," i.e. Jesus' verbal ministry. The Word answers
in terms of his words: "I have spoken openly (παρρησίᾳ λελάληκα) to the
world. I always taught in synagogue and in the temple, where all the Jews
come together; and in secret I spoke not one thing (ἐλάλησα οὐδέν)"
(18:20).[118] What a sharp contrast with the so-called messianic secret and
the private explanations of the mysteries of God's kingdom in the Synoptics![119] Strikingly, and with the principal exception of the Upper Room
Discourse, Jesus does not instruct his disciples privately in John (4:31-38;
6:66-71; and 11:1-16 hardly consisting of theological instruction, and
6:60-65 having a mixed audience of believers and unbelievers). Even the
Upper Room Discourse may not offer a true or entire exception, for there
Jesus often instructs the disciples from a standpoint subsequent to his glo-

118. Cf. Isa 45:19 LXX: οὐκ ἐν κρυφῇ λελάληκα οὐδὲ ἐν τόπῳ γῆς
σκοτεινῷ. . . . ἐγώ εἰμι ἐγώ εἰμι κύριος λαλῶν δικαιοσύνην καὶ ἀναγγέλων ἀλήθειαν,
"I have not spoken in secret nor in a dark place of [the] earth. . . . I am, I am [the]
Lord, speaking righteousness and announcing truth."
119. Cf. William Klassen, "Παρρησία in the Johannine Corpus," in *Friendship, Flattery, and Frankness of Speech: Studies in Friendship in the New Testament
World* (ed. John T. Fitzgerald; NovTSup 82; Leiden: Brill, 1996), 243.

rification (see, e.g., 13:31: "Now has the Son of Man been glorified") even though that event has not yet happened.[120] So 18:20 encapsulates Jesus' whole ministry as a public Word. And a good Word it was: "If I have spoken badly (κακῶς), testify regarding the bad. But if well (καλῶς), why are you hitting me?" (18:23). A feisty Word, too: "Why do you ask me? Ask the ones who have heard what I said (ἐλάλησα) to them. Behold, these people know the things that I said (εἶπον)" (18:21). So far from taciturnity is this Word that a servant standing by gives him a slap (18:22).

To Pilate's amazement in Mark 15:3-5 par. Matt 27:12-14, Jesus does not answer one thing in response to the many accusations brought against him. Similarly in Luke 23:9-10 Herod Antipas questions Jesus "in many words" (ἐν λόγοις ἱκανοῖς), but Jesus answers not one thing. In John 18:33-38a, by contrast, he engages in a fullscale dialogue with Pilate, one that starts with a question of Jesus' identity, "Are you the king of the Jews?" and ends with Jesus' answer, "You are saying that I am a king. I have been born for this purpose and I have come into the world for this purpose, that I might testify to the truth. Everyone who is of the truth hears my voice." With his voice Jesus testified to himself as the Word who is himself the truth (see 1:9-10 for the Word's coming into the world).

When Pilate, terrified by the Jews' statement that Jesus has made himself God's Son, asks Jesus, "Where are you from?" Jesus temporarily refuses to give him an answer (19:7-9). Why? Because in view of Pilate's fear, to answer this question would be to save himself, against his statement that he would lay down his life on his own initiative (10:17-18). But as soon as Pilate says, "You are not speaking (λαλεῖς) to me, are you? Do you not know that I have authority to release you and [that] I have authority to crucify you?" Jesus goes back into the word-business: "You would not have authority . . ." (19:10-11). According to John's Prologue, it is the Word who has authority (1:12). With characteristically

---

120. See the whole of Christina Hoegen-Rohls' *Der nachösterliche Johannes: Die Abschiedsreden als hermeneutischer Schlüssel zum vierten Evangelium* (WUNT 2/84; Tübingen: Mohr [Siebeck], 1996), and K. Scholtissek, "Abschied und Neue Gegenwart: Exegetische und theologische Reflexionen zur johanneischen Abschiedsrede 13,31–17,26," *ETL* 75 (1999): 341-45, with references to other, earlier literature on this phenomenon.

Johannine irony, Pilate heeds "these words" of Jesus' enemies rather than accepting Jesus' words, or Jesus as the Word of truth who has spoken to him only to hear him ask, "What is truth?" (19:13; cf. 18:38).

In contrast with the Synoptics, the two angels sitting in the tomb of Jesus do not announce to Mary Magdalene his resurrection, nor does she recognize the risen Jesus by sight; rather, by hearing him call her name (cf. 10:3-5, 14, 16). Only then can she announce to the disciples, "I have seen the Lord," whereas earlier she had mistakenly supposed and reported a transfer of Jesus' corpse (20:1-18). Contrast Matt 28:17, "And having seen him, they ['the eleven disciples'] worshipped him, but some doubted," and Luke 24:30-31, 35, "taking the bread he blessed [it] and, having broken [it], he started giving [it] to them; and their eyes were opened and they recognized him. . . . he was known by them in the breaking of the bread," and 34, "the Lord has really risen and appeared to Simon." In the Synoptics, sight and bread-breaking effect belief in Jesus' resurrection; in John it is his word that does so, as highlighted by the unnecessary and stylistically awkward placement of the editorial note, "And he told her [Mary] these things," right after a direct quotation of her statement, "I have seen the Lord." The note renews attention to Jesus' word as the trigger of her belief.[121]

121. A number of commentators interpret 20:8, "Then, therefore, the other disciple . . . saw and believed," as meaning that the beloved disciple believed in Jesus' resurrection because he saw the graveclothes Jesus had left behind. But the very next two verses say that "they [Peter and the beloved disciple] did not understand the scripture that he must rise from [the] dead" and "therefore they went away to their homes" (vv. 9-10). The conjunctive "for" (γάρ) at the start of v. 9 goes so far as to make their lack of understanding the reason for the beloved disciple's seeing and believing! We already know what he saw. What then did he believe? Not that Jesus had risen from the dead, which would not comport with the causal lack of scriptural understanding that Jesus must rise from the dead; rather, the earlier report of Mary Magdalene that Jesus' corpse must have been transferred to another location unknown to her and them (vv. 1-2). To counter that the beloved disciple believed Jesus had risen and that this belief "was grounded simply upon what he had seen at the tomb," not additionally on scripture (Barrett, *John*, 564), makes nonsense of the conjunctive "for," as though the beloved disciple believed in Jesus' resurrection *because of* scriptural ignorance as well as seeing the graveclothes. Believing in a transfer of Jesus'

Not as in the parallel Luke 24:36-43, where Jesus' word, "Peace to you," only provokes a fright that is overcome by the sight of his hands and feet, flesh and bones, and of his eating fish, in John 20:19-23 Jesus' very same word, "Peace to you," does not provoke fear, but lends joy to the sight of him. John emphasizes the doubled word of greeting with two immediate, unnecessary back references to it ("and having said this" [*bis*]). Then Jesus pronounces the Great Commission, breathes on the disciples, and bestows the Holy Spirit by saying, "Receive the Holy Spirit." Thomas's following insistence on seeing Jesus' scars leads Jesus to beatify those who believe without seeing; for though the sight of Jesus as risen is granted to Thomas, it is Jesus' word, or Jesus as the Word, that generates believing. And in 21:1-14 the disciples do not recognize Jesus by sight. It is his fulfilled word that draws recognition: "And he said to them, 'Cast the net on the right side of the boat, and you will find [fish].' Therefore they cast [it on the right side], and they were no longer able to haul it in

---

corpse because of scriptural ignorance, however, makes good sense. The differences between seeing and believing here and seeing and believing in vv. 24-29 are two: (1) There Thomas hears a true report that Jesus has risen; here the beloved disciple hears a false report that Jesus' corpse has been transferred. (2) There Thomas sees Jesus' risen body complete with the scars of crucifixion; here the beloved disciple sees only graveclothes in an otherwise empty tomb. These differences bar the way to inferring from the later verses that here the beloved disciple believes Jesus has risen. Brown (*John* 2:987) describes as "trite" a belief in the transfer of Jesus' corpse. But not only is this description narratively myopic; it also overlooks inferior believing elsewhere in John (see 2:23-25; 8:31-38; 11:42-43; cf. 6:66). And saying that the ignorance of scripture contradicts the beloved disciple's believing because the ignorance comes from a source with which the evangelist disagrees (so Rudolf Schnackenburg, *The Gospel according to St John, Volume Three: Commentary on Chapters 13–21* [trans. David Smith and G. A. Kon; Herder's Theological Commentary on the New Testament; New York: Crossroad, 1982], 312-13) makes hash of the narrative, raises a question why the evangelist included something contradictorily disagreeable without revising it, and leaves the "for"-clause without anything to explain in the present text (so that Schnackenburg resorts to suggesting an original explanation of unbelief in Jesus' resurrection on the part of Mary Magdalene and Peter despite their having inspected the empty tomb). But even under the view that at the empty tomb the beloved disciple already came to believe in Jesus' resurrection, vv. 24-29 devalue a belief that is based on seeing rather than hearing.

because of the multitude of fish. Therefore that disciple whom Jesus loved says to Peter, 'It is the Lord.'"[122]

Throughout the Gospel of John, then, Jesus the Word gives voice to the words that God his Father gave him to speak. But here a problem emerges. "The word" (ὁ λόγος) does not mean "the speaker" (ὁ λέγων), but "what is spoken" (τὸ λεγόμενον).[123] Therefore how can Jesus as a speaker be considered the Word that is spoken? By now the answer should be obvious: the words that the Father has given him to speak deal almost entirely with Jesus himself, nearly to the exclusion of the theme of God's kingdom which dominates the Synoptics, so that not only has the synoptic proclaimer become the Johannine proclaimed. *The proclaimer and the proclaimed have also become one and the same.* In John, Jesus is what *is* spoken even as he *does* the speaking.[124] The voice of the Father which twice

---

122. Cf. 1 John 1:1, where hearing precedes seeing and observing, is complemented by the Word of life as the subject matter of what is heard, and together with that Word chiastically frames the references to seeing and observing. Similarly, 1 John 1:2-3 starts with a reference to "the life," which has just been associated with "the Word," moves to the visible manifestation of the life and back to the preexistent state of being "with the Father" from the beginning (cf. John 1:1), reverts to being manifested and seen, but rests finally on being proclaimed and heard.

123. Alford, *Greek Testament,* 1:678.

124. So also Klaus Berger, *Im Anfang war Johannes: Datierung und Theologie des vierten Evangeliums* (Stuttgart: Quell, 1997), 128: "Weil Jesus selbst 'das Wort' ist, sind alle seine Worte und Taten nichts anderes als Selbstauslegung des eigensten Wortes des Schöpfers selbst. . . . Wer Gottes Wort in sich trägt, der kann nur von Gott und von sich reden" (cf. p. 132); Josef Blank, *Das Evangelium Johannes* (3 vols.; Geistliche Schriftlesung 4; Düsseldorf: Patmos, 1981), 4/1 b: 32: "im Johannesevangelium das Wort, das Jesus spricht, nicht irgendwelche 'Gegenstände' zum Bedeutung Jesu selber kreist; *ein Wort, in welchem Jesus selbst der zentrale Inhalt ist;* ein Wort also, in welchem fortgesetzt Jesus sich selbst auslegt und die Bedeutung seiner selbst erschliesst. Darum ist Jesu Wort auch in einem qualifizierten Sinn das Wort *Jesu.* Es ist das 'Wort des fleischgewordenen Wortes selbst', wie die Kirchenvätern sagen" (italics original); idem, *Krisis: Untersuchungen zur johanneischen Christologie und Eschatologie* (Freiburg im Breisgau: Lambertus, 1964), 129, echoed by Kammler, *Christologie und Eschatologie,* 127-28. Others make the same point (neglected by Harnack, "Ueber das Verhältnis," 206-8), but without noting the christological subject matter of the spoken Word: "The Logos is, indeed, spoken, but he also speaks"

in the Synoptics sounds from an open but distant heaven to identify Jesus as his beloved Son[125] changes in John to the voice of Jesus the incarnate Word, speaking on earth many, many times to identify *himself* as the Son whom God the Father loves[126] and who speaks the words of God.[127]

(R. C. H. Lenski, *The Interpretation of St. John's Gospel* [Columbus, Ohio: Wartburg, 1942], 30); "the work of Jesus the Word (λόγος) is done through words (ῥήματα)" (C. K. Barrett, "The Parallels between Acts and John," in *Exploring the Gospel of John* [ed. R. Alan Culpepper and C. Clifton Black; Louisville, Ky.: Westminster John Knox, 1996], 171); "as he [Jesus] speaks the word he is the Word" (C. H. Dodd in an oral statement reported by George R. Beasley-Murray, *John* [WBC 36; Waco, Tex.: Word, 1987], 10); "Ses paroles (λόγοι, ῥήματα) et la Parole de Dieu sont si indiscernables qu'à moins de percevoir celle-ci en celles-là, il faut renoncer à les comprendre. . . . avec quelle force Jésus s'identifie avec son message" (Braun, *Jean le Théologien,* 2:140-41).

125. Mark 1:11 (par. Matt 3:17 and Luke 3:22); 9:7 (par. Matt 17:5 and Luke 9:35).

126. John 3:35; 10:17; 15:9; 17:23, 24, 26.

127. F. Godet (*Commentary on the Gospel of John: With an Historical and Critical Introduction* [trans. Timothy Dwight; 2 vols.; New York: Funk & Wagnalls, 1886], 1:246-48) asks what sense it makes for the Word to have existed in the beginning, i.e. before the coming into existence of creatures to whom God could communicate through the Word. The sense is that John writes retrospectively from his own standpoint and that of the incarnation and prospectively from the standpoint of the preexistent Word. Otherwise λόγος has to be taken in the noncommunicative sense of "unarticulated reason," unlikely here, or in the sense of "plan" (so John Ashton, "The Transformation of Wisdom: A Study of the Prologue of John's Gospel," *NTS* 32 [1986]: 172-75). "Plan" fails to connect with the divine exegete in 1:18 as well as with Jesus' speech, voice, word, words, testimony, commandment, and commandments throughout the rest of John. Nor does a presentation of Jesus as Wisdom in terms of the Word link up very illuminatingly with those Johannine emphases. A presentation of Jesus as the Word in opposition to Wisdom offers a more illuminating possibility.

CHAPTER 2

The Sectarian

A t this point Wayne A. Meeks weighs in with an observation that
might be understood as driving a wedge between Jesus the Word in
John's Prologue and Jesus' words in the rest of the Gospel:

> "Logos," the loaded word that meets us in the beginning, seems to
> promise to Greek cultural sensibilities talk of reason and communica-
> tion. . . . Yet the Logos who takes flesh in the narrative is not a model
> of rationality and communication, but one who demands that follow-
> ers "abide in *my logos*," a logos that overthrows ordinary rationality,
> and by riddle, metaphor, irony, and double entendre exuberantly
> eludes straightforward communication.[1]

The qualifications "ordinary" and "straightforward" allow the Word of
the Prologue to communicate in the following narrative through words of
an extraordinary and indirect sort, but Meeks' statement overlooks a
wealth of perfectly ordinary, straightforward words in addition to the rid-

---

1. Wayne A. Meeks, "The Ethics of the Fourth Evangelist," in *Exploring the
Gospel of John* (ed. R. Alan Culpepper and C. Clifton Black; Louisville, Ky.: West-
minster John Knox, 1996), 319 (italics original); see also idem, "The Man from
Heaven in Johannine Sectarianism," *JBL* 91 (1972): 68-71.

dles, metaphors, irony, and double entendre, John 3:16 providing the most famous example. The truths that these words communicate qualify as extraordinary, but the meanings are clear enough. Otherwise the Gospel of John would not be used so much in Christian evangelism and the nurturing of new converts. Furthermore, though characters in John's narrative are often mystified by Jesus' words, the Johannine context clarifies those words for the elect in John's audience.[2]

Werner H. Kelber offers a more nuanced view, but one in which the Gospel of John is at war with itself:

> oral discourse, when scrutinized from orality-literary perspectives, discloses an interest in the enactment of *logoi* and more *logoi,* and not in their reduction to the single *Logos.* . . . What characterizes the world of oral discourse [i.e., Jesus' world] is plurality not protology, and diversity not logocentricity. In the beginning were the words.[3]

And again:

> In his capacity as the incarnate Λόγος he [Jesus] delivers a preponderance of λόγοι. . . . the privileging of the λόγος, this logocentric reduc-

2. See Stephen C. Barton, "Early Christianity and the Sociology of the Sect," in *The Open Text: New Directions for Biblical Studies?* (ed. F. Watson; London: SCM, 1993), 147-48; idem, "Historical Criticism and Social-Scientific Perspectives in New Testament Study," in *Hearing the New Testament* (ed. Joel B. Green; Grand Rapids, Mich.: Eerdmans, 1995), 75 (esp. against Meeks' further notion that riddle and misunderstanding in John do not advance the theology of revelation, discernment, and election so much as they exclude outsiders and sustain insiders socially — though they do the latter, too, I might add); Klaus Berger, *Exegese des Neuen Testaments: Neue Wege vom Text zur Auslegung* (2d ed.; Uni-Taschenbücher 658; Heidelberg: Quelle & Meyer, 1984), 230-31. Berger does wrong, however, to use the perspicuity of John's text as evidence against the sectarianism of John that I am about to discuss. The meaning of a sectarian message is clear to the elect (also against several authors in *"What Is John?" Readers and Readings of the Fourth Gospel* [ed. Fernando F. Segovia; SBLSymS 3; Atlanta: Scholars Press, 1996]).

3. Kelber, "Narrative Displacement of the Logos," 74 (see pp. 69-98 for the whole article).

tion of the λόγοι to the Λόγος, was inspired by écriture [so that the Λόγος] stands exposed as a textually reinvented, monumentalized authority. . . . [but its] coming into the world [1:9c] administers decentering, a deconstruction of its own ontotheological foundation.[4]

Kelber is echoing the anti-logocentricity of Jacques Derrida.[5] Though admitting the presence of totalizing claims in John's narrative subsequent to the Prologue, Kelber tries to save John at least halfway for postmodernism by arguing that the later plurality of words decenters and deconstructs the initial, singular Word. But we have noted the synonymous interchange of the singular and plural throughout the Fourth Gospel, so that when the Word speaks words, he speaks the word and — given himself as the primary subject matter of his speech — he speaks the Word.

Kelber fails to see that John as a whole, not just the Prologue and not just parts of the following narrative, presents a metanarrative that superimposes the Word on the words. Word-Christology gives this narrative coherence, so that the narrative engages in centering, not decentering, in construction, not deconstruction. It encompasses all time and eternity. It starts at the beginning, when the Word was already with God, and ends unendingly in eternal life with God and the Word, or in eternal judgment without them. It takes in all space as well as all time, the things above and those below, and all that exists in space and time. No fragmented or fragmenting narrative here! It is a totalizing narrative, thoroughly logocentric, though not in the sense of reliance on autonomous human reason, against which reliance postmodernists have rightly reacted.[6]

---

4. Werner H. Kelber, "The Birth of a Beginning: John 1.1-18," in *The Gospel of John as Literature: An Anthology of Twentieth-Century Perspectives* (NTTS 17; Leiden: Brill, 1993), 214, 218-19; cf. idem, "Die Fleischwerdung des Wortes in der Körperlichkeit des Textes," 31-42, esp. 40-41.

5. See esp. Kelber, "The Authority of the Word in St. John's Gospel," 119-29.

6. Cf. Meeks, "Man from Heaven," 70-71 ("Faith in Jesus, in the Fourth Gospel, . . . means transfer to a community which has totalistic and exclusive claims"); and the subsection titled "The Universal Cosmic Significance of the Logos" in Strecker's *Theology of the New Testament*, 476-77, though Strecker does not pit the

Meek's and Kelber's line is taken to what can only be described as a ridiculous extreme by Patrick Chatelion Counet, who criticizes Kelber for half measures in his interpretation of John and whose thesis reads that "John's Gospel in Jesus' words bears witness to the unsayable character of the revelation." It is not merely that the Fourth Gospel can be deconstructed by a present-day interpreter, according to Counet, but that John the evangelist himself makes Jesus deconstruct his disciples' attempts "to put the truth in a formula," i.e. in "instruments which are not good enough to truly verbalise the revelation of truth." In other words, "Jesus deals with the logocentrism of his disciples. . . . the communicative intention of language is given up by Jesus/John in favour of a non-communicative apophatic speech. . . . logocentric confessions of the disciples are negated by Jesus," so that he and John are postmodernists ahead of time. "I believe," says Counet, "that the Fourth Gospel is about the fact that truth is not a matter of language, that language is in fact an obstacle and that one must get away from language in order to reach truth."[7] Unfortunately for this thesis, John presents Jesus as the Logos who exegeted God and

---

universal cosmological meaning of the Word against postmodern fragmentation of truth. Also recognizing the totalizing character of John's narrative is Fernando F. Segovia ("The Gospel at the Close of the Century: Engagement from the Diaspora," in *"What Is John?" Readers and Readings of the Fourth Gospel* [ed. Fernando F. Segovia; SBLSymS 3; Atlanta: Scholars Press, 1996], 215), though he finds it repellant. In the same volume R. Alan Culpepper ("The Gospel of John as a Document of Faith in a Pluralistic Culture," pp. 121-25) recognizes some totalization in John but argues that "because the Gospel presents Jesus as the incarnation who made known the work of the Logos from the creation and through all time, it undercuts the triumphalism of claims that Christendom has a monopoly on the revelation of God." This argument depends explicitly, however, on a doubtful understanding of 1:9-13 as referring to the preincarnate work of the Logos as Wisdom working in all segments of the human race. A Johannine presentation of Jesus as the Logos over against Wisdom, as argued persuasively by Petersen (see below), and a reference in 1:9-13 to the incarnate ministry of the Logos demolish Culpepper's argument and leave John's totalizing narrative intact.

7. Patrick Chatelion Counet, *John, a Postmodern Gospel: Introduction to Deconstructive Exegesis Applied to the Fourth Gospel* (Biblical Interpretation Series 44; Leiden: Brill, 2000), 47, 175-77, 180, 187, 198, 257 et passim; see 320-23 for criticisms of Kelber.

whose word and words enable believers, the elect, to know God truly. Knowing God through the truth of Jesus' verbal communication is, in fact, a prominent theme in Johannine theology (6:69; 7:17; 10:14, 38; 14:7, 20; 17:3, 7, 8, 25; 1-2 John passim, plus passages too numerous to list on the theme of truth).

If the words of the Word seem obscure, they seem so only to the nonelect, unbelievers, as the Gospel itself repeatedly indicates: "And the darkness did not comprehend it [the light of the Word of life]" (1:5); "no one is able to come to me unless the Father who sent me draws that person. . . . no one is able to come to me unless it has been given to that person from the Father" (6:44, 65); "Why do you not understand (γινώσκετε) my speech (λαλιάν)? Because you are not able to hear my word (λόγον). . . . On account of this you do not hear, because you are not of God" (8:43, 47); "you do not believe, because you are not of my sheep" (10:26).

On the other hand, the elect, believers, do hear and understand: "All that the Father gives me will come to me. . . . 'And they will all be taught by God.' Everyone who has heard from the Father and learned comes to me" (6:37, 45); "the person who is of God hears the words (ῥήματα) of God" (8:47); "the sheep hear his [Jesus'] voice. . . . they know his voice. . . . my ['sheep'] know me. . . . my sheep hear my voice" (10:3, 4, 14, 27); "from now on you know him ['the Father']. . . . you know him ['the Spirit of truth'] . . . . you will know that I am in my Father, and you in me, and I in you. . . . he ['the Holy Spirit'] will teach you all things" (14:7, 17, 20, 26); "all things that I heard from my Father I made known to you" (15:15); "he ['the Spirit of truth'] will guide you into all the truth . . . and report to you the things to come. . . . he will take from mine and announce [it] to you. . . . Now we know" (16:13, 15, 30); "Now they have come to know. . . . they understood truly . . . . I made known to them your [the Father's] name, and I will make [it] known" (17:7-8, 26); "everyone who is of the truth hears my voice" (18:37).

Meeks, Kelber, and Counet fail to take account of this distinction between the elect and the nonelect, believers and unbelievers. Trond Skard Dokka notes the distinction between believers' understanding and unbelievers' misunderstanding but also notes that in John unbelievers sometimes understand and believers sometimes do not.[8] The passages quoted above, however, show that believers come to understand what at first they did not, and that unbelievers never understand the words of Jesus as salvific, or understand them salvifically.[9]

The sharpness of this Johannine distinction between the elect and the nonelect arises out of sectarianism, indeed symptomizes it. In other words, John is using the antilanguage characteristic of sectarians. They define themselves over against the world, unbelievers, the nonelect. They form themselves into an antisociety that uses an antilanguage, as described by Michael A. K. Halliday:

> An anti-society is a society that is set up within another society as a conscious alternative to it. . . . An anti-language is not only parallel to an anti-society; it is in fact generated by it. . . . The anti-language is the vehicle of resocialization. . . . It is this metaphorical character that

8. Trond Skard Dokka, "Irony and Sectarianism in the Gospel of John," in *New Readings in John: Literary and Theological Perspectives: Essays from the Scandinavian Conference on the Fourth Gospel, Aarhus 1997* (ed. Johannes Nissen and Sigfred Pedersen; JSNTSup 182; Sheffield: Sheffield Academic Press, 1999), 83-107, esp. 95-107.

9. Cf. Herbert Leroy, *Rätsel und Missverständnis: Ein Beitrag zur Formgeschichte des Johannesevangeliums* (BBB 30; Bonn: Peter Hanstein, 1968), 167, 190-91; Jerome H. Neyrey, "The Sociology of Secrecy and the Fourth Gospel," in *"What Is John?"* vol. 2: *Literary and Social Readings of the Fourth Gospel* (ed. Fernando F. Segovia; SBLSymS 7; Atlanta: Scholars Press, 1998), 92-97. The foregoing statements are not meant as a judgment on Meeks, Kelber, and Counet themselves, who may or may not understand and believe John's narrative better than they let on. "The Father has given all judgment to the Son" (5:22). But the evident doctrine of election in John (see, e.g., 15:16: "You did not choose me; rather, I chose you") falsifies Meeks' denial that John's sectarianism is "rationalized . . . by a theory of predestination," just as the comprehensiveness of John's Word-Christology falsifies Meeks' denial that John's sectarianism is "rationalized by a comprehensive myth" ("Man from Heaven," 68). Marinus de Jonge (*Jesus Stranger from Heaven and Son of God: Jesus Christ and the Christians in Johannine Perspective* [SBLSBS 11; Missoula, Mont.: Scholars Press, 1977], esp. ch. 2), whose view is otherwise similar to Meeks', does not make the same denials.

defines the anti-language. . . . Much of everyday language is metaphorical in origin. . . . What distinguishes an anti-language is that it is
itself a metaphorical entity, and hence metaphorical modes of expression are the norm [cf. the normality of metaphor in John's Gos-
pel]. . . . the speakers of an anti-language are constantly striving to
maintain a counter reality that is under pressure from the established
world.[10]

The separatism of John the sectarian shows up dramatically in his
version of one of Jesus' words, "a new commandment" that the disciples
should love one another as he has loved them.[11] It is often noted that this
commandment narrows down to fellow believers the old commandment
quoted by the synoptic Jesus from the OT, "You shall love your neighbor
as [you love] yourself," in which commandment, as the parable of the

---

10. Michael A. K. Halliday, "Anti-languages," *American Anthropologist* 78
(1976): 570, 575, 578-79, 582; see pp. 570-84 for the whole article, and idem, *Language as Social Semiotic: The Social Interpretation of Language and Meaning* (London:
Edward Arnold, 1978), 164-82. Cf. John Howard Yoder, *The Priestly Kingdom: Social
Ethics as Gospel* (Notre Dame, Ind.: University of Notre Dame Press, 1984), 50-54,
for an interpretation of selected texts couched in antilanguage, though Yoder does
not describe them as such. On the antilanguage of John in particular, see Bruce J.
Malina, "The Gospel of John in Sociolinguistic Perspective," *Protocol of the Colloquy
of the Center for Hermeneutical Studies in Hellenistic and Modern Culture* (Colloquy
48; Berkeley: Center for Hermeneutical Studies, 1985): 11-17; Malina and
Rohrbaugh, *Social-Science Commentary on the Gospel of John*, 7-14, 46-48, 59-61 et
passim; Richard L. Rohrbaugh, "The Gospel of John in the Twenty-First Century,"
in *"What Is John?"* vol. 2: *Literary and Social Readings of the Fourth Gospel* (ed.
Fernando F. Segovia; SBLSymS 7; Atlanta: Scholars Press, 1998), 260-62; and the
whole of Petersen's *Sociology of Light*. Petersen is concerned to show that John's language opposes rather than appropriates Wisdom in that antilanguage appropriates
the everyday language of a dominant society, but in such a way that the usual references do not hold. Both Petersen and Malina and Rohrbaugh connect the
antilangauge of John with his being "antisociety." See further the extended endnote
below, "Tension with the World as a Distinguishing Feature of Sectarianism."
11. John 13:34-35; 15:12-13, 17; cf. 1 John 2:10; 3:10-11, 14, 18, 23; 4:7-8,
11-12, 19-21; 5:1-2; 2 John 5.

Good Samaritan illustrates, neighborliness knows no limits.[12] Much more does the new commandment in John narrow down the commandment by which the synoptic Jesus broadens the commandment to love your neighbor to include even the loving of your enemies.[13] Though the standard of loving has escalated in John from everybody's preservative self-love to Jesus' mortally self-sacrificial love, that escalation is matched by a shrinking of the love-commandment to mutual love within the bounds of Christian community.

It does no good to appeal to John 3:16, "For God so loved the world that he gave his unique Son" (cf. 3:17; 4:42; 6:33, 51; 12:46-47), and to infer that since the Johannine Jesus sends his disciples as the Father sent him (17:18; 20:21), Christians are to love the unbelievers who in John make up "the world."[14] That in John "the world" commonly, though not always, consists of unbelievers is evident from statements and phrases such as the following: "the world did not recognize him" (1:10); "the sin of the world" (1:29); "the world . . . in order that everyone believing in him" (3:16); and so on.[15] Here, only God loves the world. Not even his

---

12. Lev 19:18; Mark 12:31 (par. Matt 22:39 and Luke 10:27); Matt 5:43; 19:19.

13. Matt 5:44 par. Luke 6:27, 35.

14. So, e.g., Hans-Josef Klauck, "Brudermord und Bruderliebe: Ethische Paradigmen in 1 Joh 3,11-17," in *Neues Testament und Ethik* (ed. Helmut Merklein; Freiburg: Herder, 1989), 151-69; Klaus Wengst, *Bedrängte Gemeinde und verherrlichter Christus: Der historische Ort des Johannesevangeliums als Schlüssel zu seiner Interpretation* (Biblisch-Theologische Studien 5; Neukirchen-Vluyn: Neukirchener Verlag, 1981), 120-30; David Wenham, "The Enigma of the Fourth Gospel: Another Look," in *Understanding, Studying and Reading* (ed. Christopher Rowland and Crispin H. T. Fletcher-Louis; JSNTSup 153; Sheffield: Sheffield Academic Press, 1998), 115; Klaus Berger, *Theologiegeschichte des Urchristentums: Theologie des Neuen Testaments* (2d ed.; Tübingen: Francke, 1995), 273-74.

15. The attempt of Malina and Rohrbaugh (*Social-Science Commentary on the Gospel of John*, 245-46) to limit "the world" in John to Israel, most especially to that portion of Israel living in Judea, fails. For it would be passing strange for Samaritan believers to exclaim concerning Jesus, as they did, "This one is truly the Savior of the world" (4:42), if they had not been part of the world, and likewise strange for Jesus to use the sun, "the light of this world" (10:9), as a metaphor for himself if unlike the sun he was shining only on Israel (8:12; 9:5; 12:46). We may omit other considerations.

Son Jesus is said to love the world of unbelievers, though John often portrays Jesus as loving believers.[16] In the Synoptics, by contrast, the only one Jesus is said to have loved, a rich man, refused discipleship (Mark 10:21). The Jesus of John does not even eat with worldlings — tax collectors, sinners, and Pharisees — as the synoptic Jesus famously does.[17] Naturally, then, the charge that Jesus is a glutton and winebibber makes no appearance in John's Gospel. In this Gospel Jesus eats only with those whom the Father has given him out of the world: in Bethany with Lazarus, in the Upper Room with his "friends" (15:13-15), and possibly with some of them again at the Sea of Tiberias (its being unclear whether he joined them in eating the breakfast he had prepared there).[18] Far from eating with worldlings and loving the world, the Johannine Jesus reveals himself to his disciples but "not to the world" (14:22) and even makes a point of not praying for the world: "I am not making request for the world, but for those you have given me ['out of the world']" (17:9 with 17:6). It would have been one thing for Jesus to have prayed for his disciples and simply omitted the world. But for him to make the point explicit that he does not pray for the world — ouch!

According to John A. T. Robinson, Jesus' not praying for the world does not imply that he fails to love the world "any more than when he says he will not disclose himself to the world but only to them ['his disciples'] (14:22): for that depends on their love for him, not his for them (14:21)."[19] Several things are wrong with this argument: (1) It misses the point that though the Jesus of John is often said to love his disciples, he is never said to love anyone who is of the world. (2) So far as we can tell from John's text, Jesus was sent as an expression of God's love for the world, not of his own love for it. (3) John might reply to Robinson that Jesus did not

16. John 11:3, 5, 36; 13:1, 23, 34; 14:21; 15:9, 10, 12; 19:26; 20:2; 21:7, 20.

17. Mark 2:16; Matt 9:11; 11:19; Luke 5:30; 7:34, 36; 14:1; 15:1-2; contrast also Paul's allowance of eating with unbelievers (1 Cor 10:27).

18. See 12:1-8; 13:1-30; 21:1-14. In the one seeming exception, Jesus' attendance at a wedding in Cana (2:1-11), he shows up only to perform a sign. Nothing is said about his eating or drinking on the occasion.

19. John A. T. Robinson, *The Priority of John* (ed. J. F. Coakley; London: SCM, 1985), 334.

pray for the world, and therefore did not love it, because the world did not love him as an expression of God's love for it. (4) In context the parallel passage cited by Robinson, i.e. 14:21-22, favors exclusion of the world rather than its inclusion (see esp. 14:19: "Yet a little while and the world sees me no longer, but you see me" — taking the present tense of the verbs as futuristic because of "yet a little while" and because of the future tense of following verbs, "will live," "will know," "will be loved," "will love," and "will disclose"). Jesus will not disclose himself to the world as he will to the disciples. Robinson is correct to say that Jesus came to save the world, but God's purpose of saving it through Jesus does not entail Jesus' loving it.

As Jesus says explicitly that he does not pray for the world, so 1 John 5:16-17 goes out of its way to deny an exhortation that one should pray for a brother who sins a sin unto death, i.e. apostatizes, and thus shows himself to be a worldling.[20] And again in 1 John, generally recognized to have been written in circumstances related to those of John's Gospel, believers are prohibited from loving the world: "Do not love the world, neither the things in the world" (2:15-17). "The things in the world" are distinguished from yet associated with "the world." Those things — "the lust of the flesh, the lust of the eyes, and the pride of livelihood" — characterize human beings. The world that "is passing away" in v. 17 stands in antithetic parallelism with the person who does God's will. First John 2:2 has just recently referenced "the whole world's sins" in contradistinction to the sins of believers. And the world that God loved in John 3:16 consists of people. Therefore "the world" that Christians are not to love in 1 John 2:15-17 likewise consists of people.[21] In our parlance, then, "do

---

20. Cf. Heinz Dietrich Wendland, *Ethik des Neuen Testaments: Eine Einführung* (GNT: NTD, Ergänzungsreihe 4; Göttingen: Vandenhoeck & Ruprecht, 1970), 115.

21. Against Robinson (*Priority*, 334), who defines the world in the impersonal terms of its allurements to avoid a prohibition of loving the worldlings who have succumbed to those allurements (among others, see also Rudolf Schnackenburg, *The Johannine Epistles: Introduction and Commentary* [trans. Reginald and Ilse Fuller; New York: Crossroad, 1992], 126: "The world that the reader should not love is not the human world but the material world . . ."). For further criticism of Robinson's multiple arguments, see the extended endnote below, "The Restriction of Love to Fellow Believers in First John."

not love the world" means "do not love non-Christians." Since the world of unbelievers includes heretics who, though professing Christian belief, "went out from us but were not of us," not loving the world entails not praying for the heretics.[22]

Just as Jesus the Word spoke God's word to the world, then, so Jesus' disciples are to do. But they are not to love the unbelieving world any more than Jesus did, or to pray for that world any more than he did (contrast Jesus' praying for his enemies and telling the disciples to pray for theirs in Matt 5:44 par. Luke 6:28, and Luke 23:34). It is enough to love one another and dangerous to love worldlings.[23] John has not gone so far

22. See 1 John 2:18-19, 22-23; 4:1-6. Horst Balz ("Johanneische Theologie und Ethik im Licht der 'letzten Stunde,'" in *Studien zum Text und zur Ethik des Neuen Testaments* [ed. Wolfgang Schrage; Berlin: Walter de Gruyter, 1986], 35-56) describes the seceders in 1 John as world-affirming. This description fits the thesis of Michael Allen Williams (*Rethinking "Gnosticism": An Argument for Dismantling a Dubious Category* [Princeton, N.J.: Princeton University Press, 1996], 96-115) that a significant proportion of so-called "Gnostics" (against whom 1 John was aimed) were not world-rejecters, as they have been traditionally described, but world-embracers. Williams suggests that they broke away in reaction against too much world-rejection by other Christians (cf. the occasionally early breakaway of a church movement from a sect, as opposed to the usually later breakaway of sects from mainline churches).

According to Willi Marxsen (*New Testament Foundations for Christian Ethics* [trans. O. C. Dean Jr.; Minneapolis: Fortress, 1993], 285, 299-309), the ethic of 1 John differs fundamentally from that of John in that 1 John uses correct Christology intellectualizingly to exclude heretics. John does not, Marxsen apparently means us to infer. John does not prohibit Christians outright from loving the world, as 1 John does. But John has moved in the direction of that prohibition, and to deny that John excludes heretics on the intellectual ground of Christology overlooks much evidence to the contrary (see Udo Schnelle, *Antidocetic Christology in the Gospel of John: An Investigation of the Place of the Fourth Gospel in the Johannine School* [trans. Linda M. Maloney; Minneapolis: Fortress, 1992]), and also the christological apostasy of many of Jesus' disciples in John 6:60-71. For sectarian traits in the Apocalypse of John, see John E. Stanley, "The Apocalypse and Contemporary Sect Analysis," in *SBL Seminar Papers, 1986* (SBLSP 25; Atlanta: Scholars Press, 1986), 412-21.

23. Against the simplistic statement of Johannes Nissen, "Community and Ethics in the Gospel of John," in *New Readings in John: Literary and Theological Perspectives: Essays from the Scandinavian Conference on the Fourth Gospel, Aarhus 1997* (ed. Johannes Nissen and Sigfred Pederson; JSNTSup 182; Sheffield: Sheffield Aca-

as the community at Qumran, who were to hate outsiders (1QS 1:10; 2:4-9; 1QM 4:1-4).[24] But he has gone so far as to have Jesus say that the gaining of "eternal life" (ζωὴν αἰώνιον) requires a person to "hate his or her life (τὴν ψυχὴν αὐτοῦ) in this world" (John 12:25), and thus to merit a description of him and his community as sectarian, so sectarian, in fact, that to enter the kingdom of God you have to be born all over again, from above, of the Spirit. Believers constitute a new species, so that loving their own kind does not entail loving those born only once, from below, of the flesh. Yet they do love their own kind. As sociologists have observed, sectarians resocialize their converts, enjoy close fellowship within their community,[25] and "have a higher proportion of their friends located within their local church."[26]

---

demic Press, 1999), 211: "The argument that John *restricts* love to members of the community is finally an argument from silence." Also arguing against restriction is Marxsen (*Foundations,* 286-90), who says that since love is always reciprocal in John, for Christians love exists as a matter of fact only in their community; but it is not that love *should* exist only in their community. Unfortunately for this argument, love is *not* always reciprocal in John; for God loved the world even though the world did not love him in return. On target is the statement by J. T. Sanders, *Ethics in the New Testament* (Philadelphia: Fortress, 1975), 92: "Since John almost certainly knew synoptic tradition and altered it significantly and not a few times, it appears he *intended* a narrowing by changing neighbor to one another."

24. Cf. the contrast between self-exclusion in 4QMMT and exclusion by unbelieving Jews in John 9:22; 12:42; 16:2. For parallels betweeen John and the community at Qumran, however, see Philip F. Esler, *The First Christians in Their Social Worlds: Social-Scientific Approaches to New Testament Interpretation* (London: Routledge, 1994), 70-91.

25. Nancy Tatum Ammerman, *Bible Believers: Fundamentalists in the Modern World* (New Brunswick, N.J.: Rutgers University Press, 1987), 78-79, 103-19.

26. Erich Goode, "Further Reflections on the Church-Sect Dimension," *Journal for the Scientific Study of Religion* 6 (1967): 274, with references to earlier literature on p. 270nn.1-2; Bryan R. Wilson, *Religion in Sociological Perspective* (Oxford: Oxford University Press, 1982), 118-20; cf. Keith A. Roberts, *Religion in Sociological Perspective* (The Dorsey Series in Sociology; Homewood, Ill.: Dorsey, 1984), 143-44. See also Dean D. Knudsen, John R. Earle, and Donald W. Shriver Jr. ("The Conception of Sectarian Religion: An Effort at Clarification," *Review of Religious Research* 20 [1978-79]: 44-60), who make exclusivity of a membership based on personal reli-

Other elements in John corroborate the sectarianism exhibited in this narrowed scope of love. John not only leaves the world outside the scope of Jesus' praying and loving and of believers' loving. He also describes the world as full of sin; as ignorant of God, God's Son, and God's children; as opposed to and hateful of God's Son and God's children; as rejoicing over Jesus' death; as dominated by Satan; and as subject to God's wrath, so that God's loving the world does not make for a partly positive view of it.[27] Rather, God loved it and Christ died for it in spite of its evil character. What comes out is the magnitude of God's love, not a partly positive view of the world.[28] (In the one Gospel that mentions the incarnation, then, the world looks wholly negative, so that we must kiss good-bye to the incarnational argument for Christians' so-called cultural mandate — against Robert Webber, who to support Christ-for-culture in that "the church is identified with the world" combines the incarnation, which among the Gospels appears only in John, with Jesus' eating with tax collectors and sinners, which appears only in the nonincarnational Synoptics.)[29] The Fourth Gospel is unalterably countercultural and sec-

gious experience one of the two characteristics they see as necessary to sectarianism, and Robin Scroggs ("The Earliest Christian Communities as Sectarian Movements," in *Social-Scientific Approaches to New Testament Interpretation* [ed. David G. Horrell; Edinburgh: T&T Clark, 1999], 74-75, 87-88), who notes that sects offer love and acceptance within a community. I prescind from discussing in detail the sociological causes of John's alienation from the world (cf. the comment of Petersen [*Sociology of Light*, 153nn.2-3] that what counts for the interpretation of John is John's perception of the social situation regardless of the accurancy of his perception), but see the extended endnote below, "Questions about the Sociological Causes of John's Alienation from the World and about Antisemitism in John."

27. John 1:10, 29; 7:7; 12:31; 14:30; 15:18; 16:8, 11, 20, 33; 17:25; see also 1 John 2:2, 15-17; 3:1; 4:1-3; 5:19.

28. Against Klauck, "Brudermord und Bruderliebe," 160, and N. H. Cassem, "A Grammatical and Contextual Inventory of the Use of κόσμος in the Johannine Corpus with Some Implications for Cosmic Theology," *NTS* 19 (1972-73): 81-91. Cassem does, however, give a fair representation of John's negativity toward the world.

29. Robert Webber, *Ancient-Future Faith: Rethinking Evangelicalism for a Postmodern World* (A Bridgepoint Book; Grand Rapids, Mich.: Baker, 1999), 169. See also idem, *The Church in the World: Opposition, Tension, or Transformation?* (Academie Books; Grand Rapids, Mich.: Zondervan, 1986), 270, and John Drury

tarian, for "a sect is a religious group that rejects the social environment in which it exists."[30]

But John's sectarianism does not stop with a wholesale denigration of the world. He also puts forward a strong doctrine of election, already noted in connection with antilanguage but here seen to go hand in glove with a limitation of Christians' love to the elect, those on whom God's love has proved effective. "A sect sees itself as a fellowship of the elect — that is, an embodiment of true believers."[31] Associated with election are the dualisms of above versus below, Spirit versus flesh, truth versus falsehood, and light versus darkness. Permeating these dualisms — here we come back to antilanguage, or an aspect thereof — is the further element of

(*Painting the Word: Christian Pictures and Their Meanings* [New Haven, Conn.: Yale University Press, 1999], 42), who after denying Word-Christology past John's Prologue states that "the incarnation of the Word is a charter for the painter's task of transforming the words of scripture into figures"; cf. Arthur F. Holmes, *The Idea of a Christian College* (2d ed.; Grand Rapids, Mich.: Eerdmans, 1987), 20; Mark A. Noll, *The Scandal of the Evangelical Mind* (Grand Rapids, Mich.: Eerdmans, 1994), 252. Webber's argument examples the danger of systematizing not only in such a way that the distinctiveness of various theological voices in the Bible is lost, but also in such a way that their homogenization produces contradictions of those voices. In fairness to Webber, however, it should be said that his larger view is eclectic.

30. Benton Johnson, "On Church and Sect," *American Sociological Review* 28 (1963): 542. Cf. Bryan R. Wilson's calling a sect's "response to the world" the "central criterion" of sect-typology ("A Typology of Sects," *Sociology of Religion: Selected Readings* [ed. Roland Robertson; New York: Penguin, 1969], 363).

31. Ronald L. Johnstone, *Religion in Society: A Sociology of Religion* (5th ed.; Upper Saddle River, N.J.: Prentice-Hall, 1997), 88. A sociologically strong doctrine of election does not imply that the sectarians holding it reject the free will of human beings; rather, they regard themselves as God's true people, chosen by him, whether or not an exercise of human will had anything to do with their election. On the presence in John of both election and free will, see Donald A. Carson, *Divine Sovereignty and Human Responsibility: Biblical Perspectives in Tension* (New Foundations Theological Library; Atlanta: John Knox, 1980), 125-98. For a comparison of election in John and that in the sectarian literature from Qumran, see Aage Pilgaard, "The Qumran Scrolls and John's Gospel," in *New Readings in John: Literary and Theological Perspectives: Essays from the Scandinavian Conference on the Fourth Gospel, Aarhus 1997* (ed. Johannes Nissen and Sigfred Pedersen; JSNTSup 182; Sheffield: Sheffield Academic Press, 1999), 130-33.

irony, i.e. language that carries an inner, correct meaning for the elect but an outer, inadequate, or wrong meaning for the nonelect. Such language reinforces John's sectarianism.[32] These elements are commonly recognized.

Not commonly recognized is a concentration on Satan at the expense of demons. We often hear that exorcisms have disappeared from John as compared with the Synoptics. The many pre-passion exorcisms that the Synoptics narrate and mention have indeed disappeared, but only to introduce and spotlight the grandest exorcism of all, that of Satan: "Now is the judgment of this world; now the ruler of this world will be cast out (ἐκβληθήσεται)" (12:31). Exorcistic language if there ever was such language! John does not dismiss exorcisms, then; he capitalizes them (in the etymological as well as current sense of "capitalize") by making Jesus' lifting up on the cross an omnibus exorcism that casts out Satan at the same time Jesus draws to himself everyone whom the Father has given him.[33] Correspondingly, John makes the Devil the father of unbelievers en masse — the whole world of them being possessed by the archdemon — rather than dealing with possession by run-of-the-mill demons of isolated individuals such as we read about in the Synoptics: "You are of [your] father the Devil, and you want to do the lusts of your father" (8:44).[34] Even one of the twelve, Judas Iscariot, is a devil whose actions are determined by the Devil (6:70; 13:2, 27; cf. the prominence of the Devil, Satan, in 1 John and the Apocalypse of John).

Thus, sectarianism has bred in John an antilanguage that blasts the Devil, satanizes the world, and impugns the flesh.[35] Paradoxically, the

---

32. Dokka, "Irony and Sectarianism," 83-108.

33. John 6:39, 65; 10:29; 12:32; 13:3(?); 17:2, 6, 7, 9, 11, 12, 24; 18:9. Cf. K. Berger, *Im Anfang war Johannes,* 170-71, and contrast Malina, "The Gospel of John in Sociolinguistic Perspective," 45, where John's supposed lack of exorcism is used to deny a classification of John as "strong group/low grid," i.e. as aiming at group- and boundary-formation.

34. To be sure, in the passage Jesus is speaking to "the Jews" (8:22, 31, 48, 52, 57), who appealed to their Abrahamic ancestry (8:33, 37, 39, 40, 52, 53, 56). But the Jews exemplify the world at large (cf. n. 15 earlier in this chapter).

35. For John's impugning of flesh that is unendued with the Spirit, see 1:13; 3:6; 6:63; 8:15.

antilanguage of John's sectarianism has bred in turn what we might call a Christology of prolanguage, i.e. Word-Christology. Appropriately, too, for it is sectarians — those who have separated from the world, who see only in black and white — it is they rather than reformers, accommodationists, and assimilationists who speak with the most controlling authority.[36] Sectarians know the truth, the whole truth, and nothing but the truth; and they know it most assuredly: "The meaning system [of a sect] claims universal validity. It seeks to interpret the universe in its totality. . . . Outside the system lies nothing but darkness and error. All other systems must be either included in itself as partial truth or relegated to intellectual damnation."[37] So it was to be expected that out of John's sectarianism should come a master narrative.

On the other hand, James M. Gustafson has attacked Christian sectarianism; and running through his attack is a correct recognition that sectarianism entails a master narrative which trumps all other narratives.[38] He is reacting against the views of George A. Lindbeck and others.[39] Lindbeck

36. Cf. the classic discussion by H. Richard Niebuhr, *Christ and Culture* (Harper Torchbooks; New York: Harper & Brothers, 1951). Niebuhr was no proponent of sectarianism, however.

37. Peter L. Berger, "The Sociological Study of Sectarianism," *Social Research* 21 (1954): 482. See also Ammerman, *Bible Believers,* 42-51; Bryan R. Wilson, *Religion in Sociological Perspective,* 91; Donald E. Miller, "Sectarianism and Secularization: The Work of Bryan Wilson," *Religious Studies Review* 5 (1979): 163; Knudsen, Earle, and Shriver, "Conception of Sectarian Religion," 44-60; and cf. the observation of Dean M. Kelley (*Why Conservative Churches Are Growing: A Study in Sociology of Religion* [New York: Harper & Row, 1972], 78-80): "Not only is theirs [the absolutists'] the only interpretation, but it explains everything," and they hold to a "belief that 'we' [referring to themselves] have the Truth and all others are in error." On evangelicals' conviction that they have the whole truth, see Christian Smith with Michael Emerson, Sally Gallagher, Paul Kennedy, and David Sikkink, *American Evangelicalism: Embattled and Thriving* (Chicago: University of Chicago Press, 1998), 126-28.

38. James M. Gustafson, "The Sectarian Temptation: Reflections on Theology, the Church and the University," *Proceedings of the Catholic Theological Society* 40 (1985): 83-94.

39. See esp. George A. Lindbeck, "The Sectarian Future of the Church," in *The God Experience: Essays in Hope* (ed. Joseph P. Whelan; The Cardinal Bea Lectures 2; New York: Newman, 1971), 226-43.

argues that the future of the church belongs to a Christianity that is sociologically sectarian, sharply distinguished from society at large, and — for all its internal diversity of class, race, theology, liturgy, and style of life — unified in making traditional Christian claims regarding the unsurpassable finality of God's revelation in Jesus Christ, which provides unique access to absolute truth. Lindbeck attenuates his allegiance to orthodox Christian tradition, however, by denying that the exclusivism of which he speaks has to conflict with "a certain kind of universalism," one that holds to God's working "redemptively" outside the church as well as within it, so that Christians must "adopt 'dialogue' rather than 'proselytism' as the appropriate form of witness."[40] Indeed, Lindbeck's attenuation is decidedly anti-sectarian and to a considerable extent betrays the rest of his rhetoric. I dare say that John would not share Lindbeck's fear of "theological sectarianism, whether of the radical or of fundamentalist and traditionalist sorts,"[41] or agree with Lindbeck's statement, "The missionary task of Christians may at times be to encourage Marxists to become better Marxists, Jews and Muslims to become better Jews and Muslims, and Buddhists to become better Buddhists."[42] More Johannine in tone is the statement of Peter Berger: "strong eruptions of religious faith have always been marked by the appearance of people with firm, unapologetic, often uncompromising convictions — that is, by types that are the very opposite of those presently engaged in the various 'relevance' operations. Put simply: Ages of faith are not marked by 'dialogue,' but by *proclamation*" (italics original).[43]

Whereas Lindbeck attenuates his sectarianism, his codefendant against Gustafson, viz., Stanley M. Hauerwas, objects to being called a sectarian, because the bad connotations of that term "shortcut" genuine argument.[44] Walter Brueggemann turns the tables by describing as sectar-

40. Ibid., 230.
41. Ibid., 237-38.
42. George A. Lindbeck, *The Nature of Doctrine: Religion and Theology in a Postliberal Age* (Philadelphia: Westminster, 1984), 54; see also 46-63.
43. Peter Berger, "A Call for Authority in the Christian Community: An Address Delivered to the 10th Plenary of the Consultation on Church Union, in Denver, Colorado," *The Christian Century* 88/43 (Oct. 27, 1971): 1262.
44. Stanley M. Hauerwas, *Christian Existence Today: Essays on Church, World,*

ian also the voice of imperialism because of its narrow interest in power as opposed to general well-being.[45] Thus "sectarian" is tossed back and forth like a hot potato. I prefer to mix metaphors by biting the bullet and swallowing the potato whole.

Back to Gustafson: his attack on sectarianism leads him to say in the interests of relativizing the Christian tradition vis-à-vis other traditions, "Jesus is not God."[46] This statement contradicts John's statement, "The Word was God" (1:1; see also 8:58; 10:30, 33; 14:9; 20:28), and illustrates the theologically as well as sociologically sectarian implications of Word-Christology.

I do not mean to say that a master narrative concerning Jesus has to carry a high Christology, much less that it has to carry a Christology of Jesus as the Word who was God. Take the Jehovah's Witnesses as an example of sectarianism having a low christology: Jesus as the word who was only a god. Sectarianism does not explain the origin of John's Word-Christology, then. Its origin remains a matter of speculation and debate, but its totalizing character goes along with sectarianism so as to create in John's case a master narrative in which the Word who was with God in the beginning was also himself God, brought into existence all things, became flesh, spoke and performed the word and words of God, divided his audience into sons of light and sons of darkness, commissioned his disciples to continue a ministry of words, returned to his preincarnate splendor, sent the Holy Spirit, and will at the last day judge the human race according to his word, i.e. according to himself. One can do no better than quote David Rensberger:

> John's high Christology thus reinforces the community's social identity, that is to say, its deprivation of identity and formation of a new identity. We can discern in this process a dialectic between the growth

---

and Living In Between (Durham, N.C.: Labyrinth, 1988), 7-8; cf. the description by Yoder (*Priestly Kingdom,* 6) of Ernst Troeltsch's using "sectarian" in a "nonpejorative technical sense" as "very peculiar."

45. Walter Brueggemann, "II Kings 18–19: The Legitimacy of a Sectarian Hermeneutic," *HBT* 7 (1985): 22-23.

46. Gustafson, "Sectarian Temptation," 93.

of high Christology and the community's disenfranchisement. It was, after all, their christological confession that apparently led to their expulsion from the synagogue. As this alienation grew, the development of a still higher Christology both expressed and compensated for their sense of loss; but the higher their Christology became, the greater grew the rift between them and synagogue Judaism.[47]

To this comment we should add that since the high Christology of John is a Christology of Jesus as the Word who, though not *of* the world, speaks volubly *to* it, John's sectarianism has sharpened rather than dulled the evangelistic thrust and usefulness — even today — of the Fourth Gospel.[48]

47. David Rensberger, *Johannine Faith and Liberating Community* (Philadelphia: Westminster, 1988), 119; cf. idem, "Sectarianism and Theological Interpretation in John," in *"What Is John?"* vol. 2: *Literary and Social Readings of the Fourth Gospel* (ed. Fernando F. Segovia: SBLSymS 7; Atlanta: Scholars Press, 1998), 146-48; Meeks, "Man from Heaven," 71; and Jerome H. Neyrey, *An Ideology of Revolt: John's Christology in Social-Science Perspective* (Philadelphia: Fortress, 1988), as a whole. Although Jack T. Sanders (*Schismatics, Sectarians, Dissidents, Deviants: The First One Hundred Years of Jewish-Christian Relations* [Valley Forge, Pa.: Trinity Press International, 1993], 92-95) doubts that Christology offers the general explanation for Jewish persecution of Christians, he makes the Johannine community an exception in this regard and sees the development of their high Christology as a result of expulsion from the synagogue. He then seems to renege, however, or at least to consider Christology an inadequate explanation, and later adopts a deviance model (pp. 129-51).

48. Contrary to Petersen (*Sociology of Light,* 81: "Their [the Johannine community's] response is not missionary fare, but the fare of communal survival"), it is wrong to pit sectarian introversion against evangelistic enterprise. Introverted sects are often the most evangelistically zealous. Think again of the Jehovah's Witnesses, also of the Mormons, and see John 20:21: "Just as the Father has sent me, I also send you." Whether a sect engages in evangelism depends on factors other than introversion, or on factors that affect the *kind* of introversion which characterizes the sect. Cf. Peter L. Berger, "Sociological Study of Sectarianism," 479, 483; Bryan R. Wilson, *The Social Dimensions of Sectarianism: Sects and New Religious Movements in Contemporary Society* (Oxford: Clarendon, 1990), 61-62; idem, *Magic and the Millennium: A Sociological Study of Religious Movements of Protest among Tribal and Third-World Peoples* (London: Heinemann, 1973), 18-26; Ammerman, *Bible Believers,* 147-66; Rensberger, *Johannine Faith and Liberating Community,* 25-29; Dokka, "Irony and Sectarianism," 104; Nissen, "Community and Ethics," 196, 200-205, 210, 212;

Marxsen, *Foundations,* 189 ("Thus loving one another takes place in a circle that is closed but not closed-*off*"); and Jonathan R. Wilson, *Living Faithfully in a Fragmented World: Lessons for the Church from MacIntyre's* After Virtue (Christian Mission and Modern Culture; Harrisburg, Pa.: Trinity Press International, 1997), 65-66 ("the church must be a community that stands over against the world for the sake of the world. . . . because the church's *telos* is to witness to God's love for the world in Jesus Christ, the church's life is also for the sake of the world"). Strangely, Klassen ("Παρρησία in the Johannine Corpus," 240) uses Jesus' boldness of speech in John to deny sectarianism, as though sectarians cannot speak boldly and must establish secret or isolated communities. Similarly, Raymond E. Brown (*The Death of the Messiah* [2 vols.; ABRL; New York: Doubleday, 1994], 1:268n.3) claims that John "has the very unsectarian outlook of Jesus insisting that he has other sheep that are not of this fold (10:16) and praying that all his followers may be one (17:20-21)" (cf. Beate Kowalski, *Die Hirtenrede [Joh 10, 1-18] im Kontext des Johannesevangeliums* [Stuttgart: Katholisches Bibelwerk, 1996], 238-39; contrast the portrayal of John's community as sectarian in Brown's *The Churches the Apostles Left Behind* [New York: Paulist, 1984], 118-23). Brown fails to take account of the fact that some, or even many, sects make far-reaching evangelistic efforts while at the same time regularly emphasizing the unity of their membership over against the world. Even Barton, who resists describing primitive Christianity in general as sectarian, admits that description of John's community in particular ("Early Christianity and the Sociology of the Sect," 141-47).

CHAPTER 3

A Paleofundamentalist Manifesto for Contemporary Evangelicalism, Especially Its Elites, in North America

I f Matthew, Mark, Luke, John, and the remaining books of the Bible offer theologies that vary according to the different circumstances in and for which these books were written (without any negative prejudice I leave aside the question of an underlying theological unity), if we accept the entirety of the Bible as canonical and therefore its various theologies as all divinely authoritative, and if it is not enough for us to know these theologies, if we must also apply them variously to circumstances like those for which they were originally tailored, then we might well ask ourselves whether we North American evangelicals are fast falling, or have already fallen, into circumstances that call for a reinstatement of John's sectarianism with its masterly, totalizing, but divisive Christology of the Word that speaks truth so incisively that as the Word, Jesus is the truth over against the father of lies, Satan, who has deceived all unbelievers. Extreme? Yes, but there are times for extremes.[1]

---

1. Cf. Niebuhr, *Christ and Culture,* 68.

Habitually, those who recognize the sectarianism of John, in particular the narrowing down of the love-commandment, minimize as much as possible that narrowing (if they do not reject it altogether) and then expatiate on its dangers. Those dangers include an isolation from the world that goes beyond separation, makes impossible an effective Christian witness to the world, and hardens the world's opposition to the gospel and oppression of the church. Other dangers often cited are a tendency to let the division of believers from unbelievers degenerate into divisiveness among believers themselves,[2] and a repression of non-Christians in the event that sectarians gain political power: "Christian universalism linked to christological exclusivism, when given the power to enforce its will, can result (and sometimes has resulted) in coercion or repression of all that refuses Christianization."[3] Even those who see in the narrowing some positive values — mutual encouragement, nonassimilation to worldly culture, and the like — overhastily stress the dangers, or hastily overstress them, rather than perceiving in general an equality of values and dangers, variations depending on particular circumstances. Rensberger, for example, describes John's sectarianism as "the defiance of a sect that has suffered exclusion itself and now hurls exclusion back in the teeth of its oppressors," yet adds, "Whether this can bear theological fruit today . . . remains problematic."[4] Richard B. Hays comes close to perceiving an equality of values and dangers, but even he considers some amelioration necessary: "exhortations for love within the community sound less exclusionary and more like an urgent appeal for unity within an oppressed minority community."[5]

2. See, e.g., Raymond E. Brown, *The Community of the Beloved Disciple* (New York: Paulist, 1979), 134-35; Rensberger, *Johannine Faith and Liberating Community*, 107-34.

3. John M. G. Barclay, "Universalism and Particularism: Twin Components of Both Judaism and Early Christianity," in *A Vision for the Church: Studies in Early Christian Ecclesiology in Honour of J. P. M. Sweet* (ed. Markus Bockmuehl and Michael B. Thompson; Edinburgh: T&T Clark, 1997), 222.

4. David Rensberger, "Sectarianism and Theological Interpretation in John," 146; see also idem, *Johannine Faith and Liberating Community*, 135-54, where it is said that John's sectarianism is not *wholly* negative but has *some* positive value.

5. Richard B. Hays, *The Moral Vision of the New Testament: A Contemporary Introduction to New Testament Ethics* (New York: HarperCollins, 1996), 145-47.

But despite its dangers and because of its values, do our circumstances call for Johannine sectarianism? On the one hand, the sociological research of Christian Smith has led him to trace the thriving of North American evangelicalism to a sense of embattlement with the world:

> American evangelicalism . . . is strong not because it is shielded against, but because it is — or at least perceives itself to be — embattled with forces that seem to oppose or threaten it. Indeed, evangelicalism . . . *thrives* on distinction, engagement, tension, conflict, and threat. Without these, evangelicalism would lose its identity and purpose and grow languid and aimless [italics original].[6]

On the other hand, the sense of embattlement with the world is rapidly evaporating among many evangelicals, especially evangelical elites, among them those who belong to "the knowledge industry." In the last half century they have enjoyed increasing success in the world of biblical and theological scholarship. They reacted against the separatism of their fundamentalist forebears, who precisely in their separation from the world knew they had from God a sure word for the world. Penetration replaced separation. Evangelical biblical and theological scholars began holding their meetings in conjunction with those of the American Academy of Religion and the Society of Biblical Literature, both of these societies populated with heretics, non-Christians of other religious persuasions, agnostics, and outright atheists as well as with true Christian believers. And in droves evangelicals (including me) started joining these societies and participating in their activities.[7] Would John approve? I do not know and maybe it does not matter whether or not he would; but noncanonically he is said to have fled from a public bath on perceiving that the heretic Cerinthus was there.[8] At the same time there is cause to celebrate that the expanding presence of evangelicals in the mainstream

6. Smith, *American Evangelicalism,* 89. For Smith's whole discussion of this point, see pp. 84-153.

7. Cf. James Davison Hunter, *Evangelicalism: The Coming Generation* (Chicago: University of Chicago Press, 1987), 46-49, 213.

8. Irenaeus, *Adv. haer.* 3.3.4.

academy and the improved quality of their scholarship have made it increasingly inexcusable and intellectually unrespectable to ignore their research and argumentation, which are now exerting much more influence than before outside the confines of evangelicalism. So I do not condemn penetration by evangelicals any more than I condemn separation by fundamentalists. Separation was necessary to save the gospel against the inroads of modernism, I think; and penetration has been necessary to save the gospel from irrelevance and a seclusion that threatened to keep it from being heard in the world at large.[9]

But what about now? What present circumstances should we evangelicals take into account? With nonevangelicals' increasing recognition of our contributions to biblical and theological scholarship and with the consequent whetting of our appetite for academic, political, and broadly cultural power and influence are coming the dangers of accommodation, of dulling the sharp edges of the gospel, of blurring the distinction between believers and the world, of softening — or not issuing at all — the warning that God's wrath abides on unbelievers (John 3:36), in short, of only whispering the Word instead of shouting him, speaking him boldly, as the Word himself did.

Besides these dangers, we have as a matter of fact — especially among liberally educated, aesthetically attuned evangelicals — a shift of emphasis from preaching to liturgy and sacrament.[10] As noted by sociolo-

9. Again see the classic discussion in Niebuhr, *Christ and Culture*. I am not unaware of the view that fundamentalism itself was a kind of modernism, particularly in its sharing historicism, and therefore evidentialism, with modernism (see, e.g., Thomas C. Oden, *After Modernity . . . What?* [Grand Rapids, Mich.: Zondervan, 1990], 66-69). But here I am using the vocabulary of fundamentalists, who called modernists those who denied historic tenets of the Christian faith.

10. See esp. Webber, *Ancient-Future Faith*, 27, 94-96, 100-101, 107-15; cf. Nathan O. Hatch and Michael S. Hamilton, "Can Evangelicalism Survive Its Success?" *Christianity Today* 36/11 (Oct. 5, 1992): 24-25. Webber argues for liturgy and sacrament, ritual and rite — which he calls "symbolic communication" with "pomp and ceremony" — on the ground that postmoderns are audiovisually oriented rather than verbally oriented or print-oriented. But the audio- may feature the verbal, indeed usually does feature it; and one wonders how Webber would explain the proliferation of large, thriving bookstores that sell a lot more than picturebooks. I should

gists of religion, this shift marks antisectarianism inasmuch as especially among conversionist sects "there is a grave distrust of ritual and rite,"[11] and inasmuch as "in the church [as opposed to a sect] . . . the spirit is remote and can be brought nearer only by formalized means."[12] So Robert Webber is correct to link his advocacy of ritual and rite with a rejection of sectarianism.[13]

But the stress of John the sectarian on verbal communication by Jesus the Word leads him to depress sacrament and liturgy. The baptism of Jesus goes unmentioned. His baptism of others is introduced only to provide an occasion for John the Baptist's testimony to Jesus' superiority as the one who "speaks the words of God" (3:22-36, esp. 34) and to be qualified as a baptizing not by Jesus himself but only through the agency of his disciples (4:1-2). Nor does John's version of the Great Commission (20:21) contain a command to carry on the practice of baptism (contrast Matt 28:19 and the emphasis in Acts on baptism in the carrying out of the Great Commission). The water in 3:5 represents the Holy Spirit as

---

add that abetting the shift to liturgy and sacrament is a sharp decline in the biblical, theological, and rhetorical quality of most preaching.

11. Donald E. Miller, "Sectarianism and Secularization," 165.

12. Peter L. Berger, "Sociological Study of Sectarianism," 480; cf. Bryan R. Wilson, *Religion in Sociological Perspective,* 98-99: "Over time, the tendency of the ministry was to reduce worship activity to more prosaic ritualized patterns." See also Max Weber, *The Protestant Ethic and the Spirit of Capitalism* (trans. Talcott Parsons; London: George Allen & Unwin, 1930), 144-54; Ernst Troeltsch, *The Social Teaching of Christian Churches* (trans. Olive Wyon; 2 vols.; New York: Macmillan, 1932), 1:338, 342; Liston Pope, *Millhands and Preachers: A Study of Gastonia* (New Haven: Yale University Press, 1942), 124; Paul Gustafson, "UO-US-PS-PO: A Restatement of Troeltsch's Church-Sect Typology," *Journal for the Scientific Study of Religion* 6 (1967): 67.

13. Webber, *Ancient-Future Faith,* 73. To the extent that Webber rejects a sectarian fragmentation of the church, I agree; but to the extent that he rejects a sectarian separation from the world, I disagree. John presses for the latter kind of separation, but stresses the unity of the church (10:16; 11:52; 17:11, 21-23) and regards heretics as split-offs who never did truly belong to apostolic Christianity (6:60-71; cf. 1 John 2:18-19; Dongsoo Kim, "The Church in the Gospel of John," *TynBul* 50 [1999]: 316-17; J. W. Pryor, "Covenant and Community in John's Gospel," *RTR* 47 [1988]: 44-47).

the agent of birth from above (cf. 7:37-39, where drinking the water that is explicitly identified with the Spirit rules out baptismal water). The wine that Jesus produced at the wedding in Cana (2:1-11) replaces the wine of the Eucharist and represents the superiority over Judaism, represented in turn by the water of Jewish purification, of the new order brought by Jesus (cf. Mark 2:22) and bought at the cost of the blood that flowed from his pierced side (John 19:34). And despite John's devotion of several chapters to the Last Supper he omits the Institution of the Lord's Supper and transmutes the Words of Institution into metaphors for the life- and Spirit-giving benefit of believing Jesus' words (6:52-65).[14]

Accompanying the un- if not anti-Johannine shift to sacramentalism and liturgy among a growing number of evangelicals are a curtailment of the doctrine of eternal punishment;[15] a migration from exclusivism to

14. See Paul N. Anderson, *The Christology of the Fourth Gospel: Its Unity and Disunity in the Light of John 6* (Valley Forge, Pa.: Trinity Press International, 1996), 110-36, with an extensive bibliography on pp. 291-93, to which should be added John Painter, "Johannine Symbols: A Case Study in Epistemology," *JTSA* 27 (1979): 26-41; Stephen C. Barton, "The Communal Dimension of Earliest Christianity," *JTS* NS 43 (1992): 414. Barton notes John's "reinterpretation of the sacraments in the direction of a far more fundamental concern with the symbolism of belief and unbelief." Debate has raged, of course, over sacramentalism versus antisacramentalism in John.

15. I am referring to something of a trend toward annihilationism, more or less equivalent to conditional immortality. For annihilationism, see E. Earle Ellis, "New Testament Teaching on Hell," in *Eschatology in Bible and Theology: Evangelical Essays at the Dawn of a New Millennium* (ed. Kent E. Brower and Mark W. Elliott; Downers Grove, Ill.: InterVarsity, 1997), 199-219; Edward Fudge, *The Fire That Consumes: The Biblical Case for Conditional Immortality* (2d ed.; Carlisle, U.K.: Paternoster, 1994); and against annihilationism see Peter M. Head, "The Duration of Divine Judgment in the New Testament," in the aforementioned *Eschatology in Bible and Theology,* 221-27; also Donald A. Carson, *The Gagging of God: Christianity Confronts Pluralism* (Grand Rapids, Mich.: Zondervan, 1996), 515-36; Millard J. Erickson, *The Evangelical Left: Encountering Postconservative Evangelical Theology* (Grand Rapids, Mich.: Baker, 1997), 123-30. Robert A. Peterson ("Undying Worm, Unquenchable Fire," *Christianity Today* 44/12 [Oct. 23, 2000]: 30-37) traces the recent and current debate, summarizes arguments pro and con, and provides further bibliography.

inclusivism; an edging toward universalism, so that it has become acceptable in evangelical ranks to express the hope — not always a wistful hope, either, but sometimes a half expectant one — for universal salvation;[16] a cooling of missionary ardor; and a growth of worldliness.[17] The "seeker-sensitivity" of evangelicals — their practice of suiting the gospel to the felt needs of people, primarily the bourgeoisie — contributes to their numerical success but can easily sow the seeds of worldliness (broadly conceived).[18]

16. Cf. Hunter, *Evangelicalism,* 34-40, 46-49; Richard Quebedeaux, *The Worldly Evangelicals* (New York: Harper & Row, 1978), 20-21. Exclusivism is the doctrine that in the present age salvation is restricted to those who are capable of believing and do hear and believe the gospel of Christ during their earthly lifetime. Inclusivism is the doctrine that the redemptive work of Christ applies also to people who respond well to amounts of divine revelation less than a fair hearing of the gospel. Universalism is the doctrine that everybody will be saved. Of course, proponents of these views would wish to qualify and nuance them. See further the extended endnote below, "Exclusivism, Inclusivism, and Universalism in Relation to John's Gospel."

17. Hunter, *Evangelicalism,* 50-52, 56-64; Quebedeaux, *Worldly Evangelicals,* 10-24. Russell R. Dynes ("Church-Sect Typology and Socio-Economic Status," *American Sociological Review* 20 [1955]: 555-60) provides evidence for a correlation between sectarianism and low socio-economic status and between the religious establishment and high socio-economic status. Among others, see also J. Alan Winter, *Continuities in the Sociology of Religion: Creed, Congregation and Community* (New York: Harper & Row, 1977), 117-32; Roberts, *Religion in Sociological Perspective,* 239-41; William Sims Bainbridge, *The Sociology of Religious Movements* (New York: Routledge, 1997), 47-53; Peter L. Berger, "Religion and the American Future," in *The Third Century: America as a Post-Industrial Society* (ed. Seymour Martin Lipset; Stanford, Calif.: Hoover Institution Press, 1979), 66-67; Pope, *Millhands and Preachers,* 96-140.

18. By worldliness I mean not merely the disregard of fundamentalist taboos against smoking, drinking, dancing, movie-going, gambling and the like, but more expansively such matters as materialism, pleasure-seeking, indiscriminate enjoyment of salacious and violent entertainment, immodesty of dress, voyeurism, sexual laxity, and divorce (cf. "the lust of the flesh and the lust of the eyes and the pride of livelihood" in 1 John 2:16 and the world-embracers among so-called "Gnostics" — Williams, *Rethinking "Gnosticism,"* 96-115). Because of its statistical measurability, take for example the evangelical culture of divorce. As of December 21, 1999, according to the Barna Research Group, Ltd. (www.barna.org), 27% of self-described born again Christians in the United States were currently or previously divorced, as com-

How so? Well, in a society such as ours where people do not feel particularly guilty before God (though in fact they are), seeker-sensitivity — if consistently carried through — will softpedal the preaching of salvation from sin, for such preaching would not meet a felt need of people. As a result, the gospel *message* of saving, sanctifying grace reduces to a gospel *massage* of physical, psychological, and social well-being that allows worldliness to flourish. Since evangelicals fall into the category of what Bryan R. Wilson has called "a conversionist sect," i.e. one that vigorously seeks converts,[19] the Niebuhrian development from antiworldly sect to worldly church may apply especially to evangelicals; for it is only "sects less interested in recruitment or better insulated or isolated from secular forces [that] tend to retain sectarian characteristics more or less indefinitely."[20] The apparent expectation of David O. Moberg that evangelicals would resist accommodation to the world is turning out to be ill-founded.[21]

---

pared with 24% of people making no claim to have been born again. Because of the large size of the sample surveyed (3,854 adults) and its geographical distribution (covering 48 continental states), the difference in percentages "*is* statistically significant" (italics added). Perhaps yet more disturbing than the higher percentage of divorce among reborns in general is the 34% of divorced people among "those associated with non-denominational Protestant churches," for those churches are likely to be evangelical (as confirmed by the Barna Research Group). For another example, take voyeurism. It has become such a problem among evangelical Christians that *Christian Computing Magazine* recently published a Special Issue dealing with it; and absent blocking, a huge amount of Internet use at evangelical institutions of higher education is devoted to pornographic sites.

19. Bryan R. Wilson, "A Typology of Sects," 364-65; idem, "An Analysis of Sect Development," *American Sociological Review* 24 (1959): 5-6.

20. Benton Johnson, "On Church and Sect," 543. I, not Johnson, make the application to evangelicals; cf. Bryan R. Wilson, "Analysis of Sect Development," 11, 14, though he does wrong to contrast adventism — an emphasis on Jesus' return in the case of Christianity — with evangelism, for the two have gone together in evangelicalism despite a recent decline of adventism among evangelical elites.

21. David O. Moberg, "Fundamentalists and Evangelicals in Society," in *The Evangelicals: What They Believe, Who They Are, Where They Are Changing* [ed. David F. Wells and John D. Woodbridge; Nashville: Abingdon, 1975], 162-63; cf. in the same volume Martin E. Marty, "Tensions Within Contemporary Evangelicalism: A Critical Appraisal," 177-78.

In the larger culture we have an insinuation of religious syncretism by way of the multicultural movement; the incursion of religious pluralism;[22] the dominance of tolerance among American civic virtues; the breakdown of system-building and universal truth-claims in philosophy; a relegation of history to the realm of fiction; the dismantling of canonicity in many literary circles; the death of external referentiality in intertextuality; postmodern artists' abandonment of the attempt to find a universal language in color and abstraction;[23] postmodern architects' abandonment of the "International Style," governed by general laws and the universal, in favor of heterogeneity, the particular and the local;[24] indeterminacy in natural science and its ripple effect on other fields; the virtualizing of reality — what we might

22. "A CNN/USA Today/Gallup poll conducted last December [1999] showed that 75 percent of Americans do not view their religion as the only true path to God, and of that number, a substantial majority (82 percent) believe that another path to God is equally good as their own" (*Santa Barbara News-Press* [Saturday, June 3, 2000]: D4). More pertinently, according to the aforementioned Barna Research Group 34% of born again Christians believe that "if a person is generally good, or does enough good things for others during their lives, they will earn a place in heaven." In the general population this view grew 12-13% in the short period 1992-1999.

23. For this attempt, see Wassily Kandinsky, *Concerning the Spiritual in Art* (trans. M. T. H. Sadler; New York: Dover, 1977), esp. 19-20, 27-33. Typical is the statement, "Every artist, as a servant of art, has to help the cause of art (this is the element of pure artistry, *which is constant in all ages and among all nationalities*" (p. 33, italics added). Kandinsky likens the modern art of color and abstraction to what he takes to be the universal language of music. See also John Golding, *Paths to the Absolute: Mondrian, Malevich, Kandinsky, Pollock, Newman, Rothko, and Still* (The A. W. Mellon Lectures in the Fine Arts, 1997; Bollington Series 35/48; Princeton, N.J.: Princeton University Press, 2000); Herschel B. Chipp, *Theories of Modern Art: A Source Book by Artists and Critics* (Berkeley: University of California Press, 1968), 309-65; H. R. Rookmaaker, *Modern Art and the Death of a Culture* (2d ed.; Downers Grove, Ill.: Inter-Varsity Press, 1973), 110-19 and, for the breakdown of the artistic attempt to attain a universal language of color and abstraction, 119-30.

24. Heinrich Klotz, "Postmodern Architecture," in *The Post-Modern Reader* (ed. Charles Jencks; New York: St. Martin's Press, 1992), 234-48; and, in the same volume, Paolo Portoghesi, "What Is the Postmodern?" 208-14; Andreas Huyssen, "Mapping the Postmodern," 44-47; Charles Jencks, "The Post-Modern Agenda," 24-27; also David F. Wells, *No Place for Truth; or, Whatever Happened to Evangelical Theology?* (Grand Rapids, Mich.: Eerdmans, 1993), 63-65.

call its docetizing — in cyberspace;[25] the personalization of politics at the expense of ideology; and the sentimentalizing of popular culture ("How do you feel?" instead of "What do you think?" or, as the first song in Andrew Lloyd Webber's "Joseph and the Amazing Technicolor Dreamcoat" puts it, "You are what you feel," and as the last song puts it, "Any Dream Will Do"). Not that all these developments are entirely and absolutely bad, but their extremity and hegemony are enough to cause alarm.

Ian Buruma, a self-confessed secularist, speaks critically of "a new Romantic age, which is anti-rational, sentimental, and communitarian," of "historiography" as "less and less a matter of finding out how things really were, or trying to explain how things happened," of "historical truth" as "not only . . . irrelevant," but also "a common assumption that there is no such thing," of "sharing the pain of others" so that "we learn to understand their feelings, and get in touch with our own," of a situation in which "all truth is subjective, only feelings are authentic," of "politicians" who "appeal to sentiments instead of ideas," and of "the steady substitution of political argument in public life with the soothing rhetoric of healing."[26] The seeker-sensitivity of contemporary evangelicalism has produced a consumerized version of Christianity that can be understood as of a piece with this postmodern revolt of popular, mass culture against high modernism (cf. the kitsch and schlock of much Christian television).[27]

---

25. For *anti*docetism in John, see Schnelle, *Antidocetic Christology*, and Howard M. Jackson, "Ancient Self-Referential Conventions and Their Implications for the Authorship and Integrity of the Gospel of John," *JTS* NS 50 (1999): 18-19. M. J. J. Menken ("The Christology of the Fourth Gospel: A Survey of Recent Research," in *From Jesus to John: Essays on Jesus and New Testament Christology in Honour of Marinus de Jonge* [ed. Martinus De Boer; JSNTSup 84; Sheffield: Sheffield Academic Press, 1993], 307-8) objects that unlike the First Epistle of John, the Gospel of John is not explicitly antidocetic. But given the difference in literary genre between a gospel and an epistle, at least the statement in John 1:14 is as antidocetic as should be expected.

26. Ian Buruma, "The Joys and Perils of Victimhood," *The New York Review of Books* 46/6 (April 8, 1999): 4, 6, 8-9.

27. On the postmodern revolt, see Andreas Huyssen, *After the Great Divide: Modernity, Mass Culture, Postmodernism* (Theories of Representation and Difference; Bloomington, Ind.: Indiana University Press, 1986).

Convinced of our immunity to these developments, we evangelicals rail against the Jesus Seminar for portraying the historical Jesus as a mere sage who tossed off wise and witty aphorisms regarding present human existence. The question of historicity apart, the Fourth Gospel offers a powerful counter to that noneschatological, present-oriented portrayal: long discourses and dialogues over against short sayings, the revelation of heavenly things over against the observation of earthly things, Christology in the service of theology over against a socioeconomic agenda in the service of anthropology, the present as a prelude to the future over against a disregard of the future in favor of the present. N.B.: *John's realized eschatology does not replace futurism with presentism; rather, it brings the eternity of the Word into the present so as to invest the present with issues of an eternal destiny yet to come* (and thus, by the way, thwarts efforts to make the Fourth Gospel a canonical companion of the Gospel of Thomas, which shows little or no interest in eternal destiny). John is so focused on eternal destiny that you do not find in his Gospel the detailed set of behavioral rules usually found in sectarian literature.[28]

But consider how much of the popular literature that stocks the shelves of evangelical Christian bookstores deals with present human existence: the youth culture, dating, romance, love, sex, marriage, parenting, divorce, remarriage, finances, diet, physical beauty, physical health, emotional health, self-development, self-esteem, success, failure, burnout, personal empowerment, leadership, friendship, conflict resolution. The present-oriented Jesus of this literature — and of most evangelical preaching, too — begins to look and sound not a little like the noneschatological, present-oriented Jesus of the Jesus Seminar, and also not a little like the self-actualization in ancient "Gnosticism" such as formed a background for Johannine literature. In evangelical scholarly and activist

---

28. On John's investing the present with issues of eternal destiny, see Jörg Frey, *Die johanneische Eschatologie*, vol. 3: *Die eschatologische Verkündigung in den johanneischen Texten* (WUNT 117; Tübingen: Mohr Siebeck, 2000), 241-462, and against Rudolf Bultmann's existentializing of Johannine eschatology, vol. 1: *Ihre Probleme im Spiegel der Forschung seit Reimarus* (WUNT 96; Tübingen: Mohr Siebeck, 1997), 103-18; also against the extreme of Kammler (*Christologie und Eschatologie*) in denying all futuristic eschatology in the Fourth Gospel.

81

circles this fixation on the present shows itself in a burgeoning stress on social ethics and public morality.[29] One could wonder whether this stress may be somewhat related to qualms over exclusivism and eternal punishment in that social ethics and public morality fill a void left by the neglect, compromise, and denial of those doctrines.

Clearly, North American evangelicalism is showing signs of movement along what sociologists call the route from sect to church. Sects break away from mainline religious institutions and seek to recapture the doctrinal and behavioral purity which according to their belief originally characterized the parent institution but which that institution has lost or seriously compromised through accommodation to the surrounding culture: "the sect is a protest group."[30] Such an accommodation takes the form of

29. On the Reformed side, see the subsection, "Stressing the Ethical," in George Marsden's *Understanding Fundamentalism and Evangelicalism* (Grand Rapids, Mich.: Eerdmans, 1991), 34-35. On the Anabaptist side, see Yoder, *Priestly Kingdom,* esp. 44, where "a missionary ethic of incarnation" takes the form — solely, so far as I can tell — of social activism (cf. idem, *The Royal Priesthood: Essays Ecclesiological and Ecumenical* [Grand Rapids, Mich.: Eerdmans, 1994], 84, 90-95). Contrast the early Anabaptist emphasis on conversion by evangelism (Franklin Hamlin Littell, *The Anabaptist View of the Church* [Boston: Starr King, 1958], 94-112; idem, "The Social Background of the Anabaptist View of the Church," in *Sociology and Religion: A Book of Readings* [ed. Norman Birnbaum and Gertrud Lenzer; Englewood Cliffs, N.J.: Prentice-Hall, 1969], 230-37; Wolfgang Schäufele, *Das missionarische Bewusstsein und Wirken der Täufer* [Beiträge zur Geschichte und Lehre der Reformierten Kirche 21; Neukirchen: Verlag des Erziehungsvereins, 1966], esp. 73-79, 97-98, 132-34, 138-39, 141-53, 176-82, 186-212; and Robert Webber, "Conservatism: Separatistic Christianity," in Marvin K. Mayers, Lawrence O. Richards, and Robert Webber, *Reshaping Evangelical Higher Education* [Grand Rapids, Mich.: Zondervan, 1972], 38-40). Yoder ("Reformation and Missions: A Literature Review," *Occasional Bulletin from the Missionary Research Library* 22/6 [June, 1971]: 1-9) discusses reasons why Anabaptists engaged in missionary work during the Reformation but the rest of the Reformers, especially Luther and Lutherans, did not.

30. Bryan R. Wilson, *Religion in Sociological Perspective,* 92. See also Johnstone, *Religion in Society,* 88; Rodney Stark and William Sims Bainbridge, *The Future of Religion: Secularization, Revival and Cult Formation* (Berkeley: University of California Press, 1985), 25, 99-125. Leaving cults out of account, it scarcely needs saying any more that church and sect represent ideal types at the extremes of a broad spec-

this-worldliness and present rewards at the expense of other-worldliness and future rewards: "When hell is gone, can heaven's departure be far behind?" ask the sociologists Roger Finke and Rodney Stark, and note that "the churching of America was accomplished by aggressive churches committed to vivid otherworldliness."[31] Naturally, it is those comparatively lacking in present rewards — economic prosperity, educational advantage, professional respect, and social standing in culture at large — who break away to form sects oriented to the hereafter, when the last will be first and the first, last. But in successful sects upward mobility accompanies growth in membership and makes the sect less and less other-worldly, more and more this-worldly. The cost of discipleship goes on sale for a discount. Zeal to rescue the perishing wanes. The rate of growth slows down, and the sect evolves into an institution that has more or less made peace with its environment. Finke and Stark hammer home these points relentlessly:

> as denominations have modernized their doctrines and embraced temporal values, they have gone into decline. . . . the message becomes more worldly, and is held with less certainty as religion becomes the focus of scholarly critique and attention. . . . [the decline in sects starts when they] begin to lift restrictions on behavior and to soften doctrines that had served to set the sect apart from its social en-

---

trum containing many actual types in between (see J. Milton Yinger, *The Scientific Study of Religion* [London: Macmillan, 1970], 251-81; Stark and Bainbridge, *Future of Religion*, 19-37; Johnstone, *Religion in Society*, 87-113 [further bibliography in n. 36 on p. 112]).

31. Roger Finke and Rodney Stark, *The Churching of America, 1776-1990: Winners and Losers in Our Religious Economy* (New Brunswick, N.J.: Rutgers University Press, 1992), 275 and 1, respectively; cf. Johnstone, *Religion in Society*, 88: "Sects tend to concentrate on other-worldly issues (salvation, deliverance, heaven, and hell) and discount or deprecate this world's concerns." See also Troeltsch, *Social Teaching*, 1:337; Pope, *Millhands and Preachers*, 123; Winter, *Continuities*, 141; Scroggs, "Earliest Christian Communities," 88; Peter L. Berger, "Religion and the American Future," 77 ("The revitalization of the religious community is an even deeper imperative [than the revitalization of the American political community], for it points beyond America *and indeed beyond history*" (italics added); and p. 67 above, however, for an attenuated sectarianism that lacks a futuristic emphasis.

vironment. . . . as the general affluence and social standing of a group rises, otherworldliness — as expressed through tension with the environment — becomes perceived as increasingly costly. . . . *religious organizations are stronger to the degree that they impose significant costs in terms of sacrifice and even stigma upon their members* [italics original].

Finke and Stark also present abundant empirical data to back up these statements.[32]

In the early twentieth century fundamentalists broke away from institutionally ensconced modernism so as to reaffirm the historic tenets of Christian faith.[33] That is to say, fundamentalism started sectarily, just as the Jesus-movement started as a sectarian breakaway from institutional Judaism, which had refused Jesus' eschatologically oriented attempt at a reformation.[34] But by mid-twentieth century a move was afoot among evangelicals (so we now call some former fundamentalists) to engage culture at large in terms of present human existence, as in Carl F. H. Henry's *The Uneasy Conscience of Modern Fundamentalism* (Grand Rapids, Mich.: Eerdmans, 1947), which called for political involvement and humanitarian activity.[35] The call was heeded (cf. the current preoccupation of evangelical institutions of higher education with presenting a respectable pub-

32. Finke and Stark, *Churching of America,* 18, 84, 150, 169, 238; cf. 249-55 and Kelley, *Why Conservative Churches Are Growing,* 47-77, 112-32.

33. For a short survey of this breakaway, see Joel A. Carpenter, "From Fundamentalism to the New Evangelical Coalition," in *Evangelicalism and Modern America* (ed. George Marsden; Grand Rapids, Mich.: Eerdmans, 1984), 3-16. For some criticisms of Carpenter's book, *Revive Us Again: The Reawakening of American Fundamentalism* (New York: Oxford University Press, 1997), see Sean Michael Lucas, "Fundamentalisms Revived and Still Standing: A Review Essay," *WTJ* 60 (1998): 327-37, esp. 329-32, 335-37. Not all his criticisms are telling, however. And for a bibliography on the history of fundamentalism and evangelicalism, see Smith, *American Evangelicalism,* 2n.2.

34. See the extended endnote below, "The Sectarian Start of Christianity."

35. See also David O. Moberg, *The Great Reversal: Evangelicalism Versus Social Concern* (Evangelical Perspectives; Philadelphia: Lippincott, 1972); cf. a broader treatment by Jon R. Stone, *On the Boundaries of American Evangelicalism: The Postwar Evangelical Coalition* (New York: St. Martin's Press, 1997).

lic image to the nonevangelical world by highlighting their students' and alumni's political involvement and humanitarian activity and by lowlighting those evangelistic activities that the world scornfully and disapprovingly calls proselytism — a preoccupation that lends some alarming credence to Hunter's observation and half-prediction: "Increased levels of tolerance . . . have been clearly related to greater educational achievement. . . . [higher] education may prove counterproductive to the survival of Protestant orthodoxy in America in the long run"[36]). Michael S. Hamilton traces the concomitant passage from fundamentalist poverty to evangelical prosperity, the proportional decrease in expenditures on saving souls for eternity, and the proportional increase of expenditure on fleshing out what used to be called "The Social Gospel":

> In the 1930s most evangelical parachurch organizations devoted themselves mainly to evangelism. But since that time, evangelical wealth has permitted the growth of a large new parachurch segment designed to deliver services to the already-converted. . . . [Take, for example,] contemporary Christian music. Those who launched the genre intended it to be evangelistic, with an audience of non-Christians. But it has since evolved into entertainment for Christians, and we now spend over $800 million on gospel music every year. . . . Evangelicals now spend vast amounts of money on social welfare and human-service activities at home and abroad. In the 1930s, most missionary agencies emphasized evangelism, church-planting, and discipleship. In 1998, however, four of the five largest overseas ministries specialized in relief, development, and education work. For many of these agencies, evangelism is a secondary concern. Evangelicals have

36. James Davison Hunter, *American Evangelicalism: Conservative Religion and the Quandary of Modernity* (New Brunswick, N.J.: Rutgers University Press, 1983), 132. On the recent increase in evangelicals' social activism, see idem, "The New Class and the Young Evangelicals," *Review of Religious Research* 22 (1980-81): 155-69; idem, "The Perils of Idealism: A Reply," *Review of Religious Research* 24 (1982-83): 267-76 (in reply to Boyd Reese, "The New Class and the Young Evangelicals — Second Thoughts," *Review of Religious Research* 24 [1982-83]: 261-67); Webber, *Church in the World,* 239-57.

also built an extensive network of domestic human-service agencies since the 1940s, including summer camps, women's centers, urban rescue missions, drug and alcohol treatment centers, daycare facilities, senior centers, homes for the disabled, prison ministries, youth programs, counseling services, and urban development initiatives. Total spending here is at least $3 billion [per annum, one presumes], and may be as much as $4 billion. This number does not include the enormous value of our volunteer time. Nor does it include the stacks of money evangelicals give to nonreligious human-services organizations. . . . Many will greet with hosannas the resurrection of evangelicalism's social conscience; others will put on sackcloth and ashes over the apparent diminishment of evangelistic outreach.[37]

Accompanying the social engagement for which Henry called (and I do not doubt that it was needed at the time) were increasing upgrades not only in the economic but also in the educational and social levels of evangelicals. The rate of evangelical church growth slowed down,[38] though that slowdown might have belonged to a trend throughout American Christianity.[39] More certainly to the point, then, behavioral standards

37. Michael S. Hamilton, "We're in the Money! How Did Evangelicals Get So Wealthy, and What Has It Done to Us?" *Christianity Today* 44/7 (June 12, 2000): 42-43, and 36-43 for the whole article. For fuller details, see Hamilton's essay, "More Money, More Ministry: The Financing of American Evangelicalism Since 1945," *More Money, More Ministry: Money and Evangelicalism in Recent North American History* (ed. Larry Eskridge and Mark A. Noll; Grand Rapids, Mich.: Eerdmans, 2000), 104-38, esp. 118-19, 130-38. Cf. Hunter, *Evangelicalism*, 40-46; David Hesselgrave, "Evangelical Mission in 2001 and Beyond — Who Will Set the Agenda?" *Trinity World Forum* 26/2 (Spring, 2001): 1-3.

38. Hunter (*Evangelicalism*, 204-206) documents a decline in the growth rate of evangelical churches 1940-83, the very period of evangelicalism's renunciation of fundamentalism. The years 1970-75 formed a slight, temporary exception to this decline.

39. David A. Roozen and C. Kirk Hadaway, *Church and Denominational Growth* (Nashville: Abingdon, 1993), 396-97; and in the same volume Roozen, "Denominations Grow as Individuals Join Congregations," 17-18. One can question, however, the inclusion and omission of certain denominations, and nondenominational churches as well, so far as the category of conservative Protestant churches is concerned.

started dropping.[40] Sermons and Bible studies began to concentrate more and more on the practicalities of Christian life in the here and now, so that today one rarely hears about heaven and hell, eternal life and eternal damnation. Concern with daily practicalities has largely crowded out interest in and knowledge of Christian doctrine. Symptomatically, the most influential evangelical is no longer an evangelist (Billy Graham), but a pyschologist (James Dobson).

Here it is worth quoting at length some observations by the sociologist James Davison Hunter:

> Today an increasingly large number of Evangelicals believe that there are alternative ways to heaven, especially for those who have not had the opportunity to hear of Jesus Christ. The difference between the traditional soteriology and this somewhat softened perspective is, from the vantage point of historical orthodoxy, very important. . . . Accordingly, views of heaven and hell are changing. Fewer and fewer Evangelicals believe in the existence of hell as an objective location and damnation as physical punishment. . . . the lessening concern [among evangelicals] with the proclamation of an objective and universal truth to a concern with the subjective applicability of truth. . . . one device among many of therapeutic self-understanding, identity construction, and personal meaning. . . . [The] traditional psychology [of self-denial] has given way to a relatively contemporary one that implicitly venerates the self. . . . How is the renunciation of the self possible if it is being "actualized" or "developed to its full-potential"? . . . In this [seeker-sensitive] movement [among evangelicals], the shopping mall becomes the paradigm of organizational effort. Marketing research is used to determine what insiders call the "felt needs" of the consumers. Rather than preaching what the traditions always held to be objectively true, ministry has now become oriented toward satisfying the psychological and emotional needs of those in the pew. Religious authority is transformed [*sic?* transferred] from external demands of the

---

40. From a fundamentalist standpoint, see *The Fundamentalist Phenomenon: The Resurgence of Conservative Christianity* (ed. Jerry Falwell with Ed Dobson and Ed Hinson; Garden City, N.Y.: Doubleday, 1981), 163-73.

institution to the internal needs of the individual. . . . In this the organizational seat of authority is no longer the church, its traditions, its
sacred texts or its leadership but the parishioner him or herself. The
consumer . . . has become sovereign. . . . [Evangelicalism] thinks it is
maintaining continuity with the historic traditions, but it is doing
so in such a way that it is gutting its tradition from the inside out.[41]

To be sure, joy, happiness and optimism have long been themes within
Protestant spirituality. Yet these things had always had an other-
worldly character to them [e.g., the joy of being saved, the hope of
reaching heaven, etc.]. This still exists in some measure. What differ-
entiates contemporary from traditional Evangelical notions of joy,
happiness, etc., [and what qualifies it as "hedonistic"] is its distinctly
inner-worldly appeal. . . . Evangelicalism has accommodated to the
subjectivism in the larger culture.[42]

[The contemporary evangelical] has either forgotten, repudiated, or
"outgrown" traditional definitions of worldliness, and . . . has made a
moral and spiritual virtue of self-understanding and self-expression.[43]

41. James Davison Hunter, "Breaking Traditions: Fin de Siècle 1896 and
1996," *Partisan Review* 64 (1997): 191-93, 212.
42. James Davison Hunter, "Subjectivization and the New Evangelical
Theodicy," *Journal for the Scientific Study of Religion* 21 (1982): 45; see also 39-47.
43. Hunter, "Breaking Traditions," 192. Robert Wuthnow (*After Heaven:
Spirituality in America since the 1950s* [Berkeley: University of California Press,
1998], 142-67) discusses recent and current spirituality as self-expression; and, as
the title indicates, issues of eternal destiny are notable by their absence so that instead of "gospel truth" we have a "gospel technology" which "some people can use to
live better lives" (p. 106). See also Hunter, *Evangelicalism,* 64-75, 157-86; idem,
"Conservative Protestantism," in *The Sacred in a Secular Age: Toward Revision in
the Scientific Study of Religion* (ed. Phillip E. Hammond; Berkeley: University of
California Press, 1985), 159-60; Phillip E. Hammond and James Davison Hunter,
"On Maintaining Plausibility: The Worldview of Evangelical College Students,"
Journal for the Scientific Study of Religion 23 (1984): 224-25; Wells, *No Place for
Truth,* 112-15, 137-86; Hatch and Hamilton, "Can Evangelicalism Survive Its Suc-
cess?" 24-25; Wade Clark Roof and William McKinney, *American Mainline Reli-
gion: Its Changing Shape and Future* (New Brunswick, N.J.: Rutgers University Press,

These observations call to mind Philip Rieff's comments: "Trained to be incapable of sustaining sectarian satisfactions, psychological man cannot be susceptible to sectarian control. Religious man was born to be saved; psychological man is born to be pleased," and "Preaching, which once communicated revelatory messages, is a dead art, wrapping empty packages in elaborate solecisms [nostrums?]."[44]

The scandal of the evangelical mind pales before the scandal of evangelical acculturation.[45] The signs are so "plain" that "he who reads

---

1987), 4, 52, 93. Matthew P. Lawson ("Sects and Churches, Conservatives and Liberals: Shades of Max Weber in the Sociology of Religion in America, 1904-1993," *Research in the Social Scientific Study of Religion* 6 [1994]: 25) has complained that Hunter "failed to distinguish between fundamentalists and mainstream evangelicals, who are quite varied in their attitudes toward the modern world." But this complaint neglects that evangelicalism has grown out of fundamentalism — the very point that Hunter made. For a full-scale investigation of soft-sell evangelicalism, see Kimon Howland Sargeant, *Seeker Churches: Promoting Traditional Religion in a Nontraditional Way* (New Brunswick, N.J.: Rutgers University Press, 2000), esp. 77-105, 163-89; and for a somewhat unsympathetic survey of laments over the Laodiceaizing of contemporary evangelicalism, see Stanley J. Grenz, *Renewing the Center: Evangelical Theology in a Post-Theological Era* (A Bridgepoint Book; Grand Rapids, Mich.: Baker, 2000), 11-15, 162-68.

44. Philip Rieff, *The Triumph of the Therapeutic: Uses of Faith After Freud* (Harper Torchbooks; New York: Harper & Row, 1966), 24, 25, 255 et passim.

45. Against Noll, *The Scandal of the Evangelical Mind*. See his p. 252: "The questions with greatest intellectual moment for those of us who are fundamentalists and evangelicals are the questions with greatest moment — period." There follows a series of questions relating salvific events to the present world and finishing with the question, "And does the Holy Spirit really extend to repentant sinners the benefits of the incarnate Christ *in this life?*" (italics added). I do not doubt that Noll believes in the importance of eternal destiny, but it seems that his distaste for evangelical non- and anti-intellectualism and his enthusiasm for evangelical intellectualism have lured him into making questions about the present life of greater moment than questions about the afterlife. Throughout his book he exhibits antagonism toward futuristic eschatological thinking, because he considers it damaging to a program of Christian influence on current culture. One can understand a reaction against the quirky eschatology of much popular evangelicalism, but how different is Noll's program from that most incarnational, indeed the only incarnational, of the canonical Gospels — the eternity-oriented, countercultural, antiworldly Gospel of John!

may run" (Hab 2:2), i.e. so plain that you can read them even on the run. North American evangelicalism is indeed travelling down Constantine Road, the road from sectarianism to mainline institutionalism. In fact, one sociologist expressed to me in conversation the opinion that historians will look back at the latter half of the twentieth century and judge evangelical churches to have been mainline, not the withering and increasingly irrelevant denominations that are popularly called mainline.[46]

The question before us is whether we can or will cut short what sociologists describe as the likely if not inevitable evolution of a successful sect into an institution through accommodation to the surrounding culture,[47] and whether John's Christology of Jesus as the Word who entered

---

46. See also Roof and McKinney, *American Mainline Religion,* 18-25, 233-34, 236-43; Michael A. Burdick and Phillip E. Hammond, "World Order and Mainline Religions: The Case of Protestant Foreign Missions," in *World Order and Religion* (ed. Wade Clark Roof; SUNY Series in Religion, Culture, and Society; Albany, N.Y.: State University of New York Press, 1991), 205: "mainline churches are no longer so mainline, and so-called sectarian churches are assuming increasingly representative status." From the other side James M. Dunn ("Fundamentalism and the American Polity: A Response," in *The Fundamentalist Phenomenon: A View from Within; A Response from Without* [ed. Norman J. Cohen; Starkoff Institute Studies in Ethics and Contemporary Moral Problems; Grand Rapids, Mich.: Eerdmans, 1990], 145) says, "We have been the mainline for many years and are just now being discovered by intensely parochially educated Easterners." Cf. Hunter, *Evangelicalism,* 6-9; Quebedeaux, *Worldly Evangelicals,* xi-xii, 3-5; Noll, *Scandal of the Evangelical Mind,* 9-10.

47. See Calvin Redekop, "The Sect Cycle in Perspective," *Mennonite Quarterly Review* 36 (1962): 155-61; Yinger, *Scientific Study of Religion,* 270, that the movement from sect to church can be reversed though, as observed by Pope (*Millhands and Preachers,* 120), "movement on the scale between sect and Church is, with minor exceptions, in one direction only [from sect to Church]" (cf. Hunter, *American Evangelicalism,* 133-34). The case of the Southern Baptist Convention may be proving a major exception, however. Literature on the evolution from sect to church is vast, but see H. Richard Niebuhr, *The Social Sources of Denominationalism* (New York: Henry Holt, 1929), 17-21; Benton Johnson, "A Critical Appraisal of Church-Sect Typology," *American Sociological Review* 22 (1957): 89; idem, "Church and Sect Revisited," *Journal for the Scientific Study of Religion* 10 (1971): 124-37; Winter, *Continuities,* 139-64; Johnstone, *Religion in Society,* 96-99.

the world of unbelievers to separate the elect, who are not of that world, from it and thus save them from the wrath of God that abides on unbelievers — whether that Christology is just the sort of message which, if recaptured, might halt our journey from vibrant sectarianism to torpid institutionalism. So I ask, are we overdosing on the this-worldly ethical, social, and psychological benefits of the gospel?[48] Is it time for some Johannine counterbalancing that puts emphasis on other-worldliness, on the final fate of human beings, and on the authoritative Word from above more than on the merely suggestive words of human counsel that most preachers minister these days? With John's relatively *a*psychological, *a*social, *an*ethical stress on the Word, is it time for evangelical elites to remind themselves of the preeminence of evangelism over private therapy, political activism, and moralistic pronouncements in the public sphere?[49] Is it time for John's anti- or at least unsacramentalism to halt our drift into the sacramentalism that characterizes institutional churches and into the liturgies that frame such sacramentalism?

I have been asked, Why turn for correction to a fundamentalistic sectarianism that entails a Johannine separation from the world? Why

48. Some of the attraction exercised on evangelicals by N. T. Wright's view of the historical Jesus as a this-worldly Jewish reformer may be due to the general this-worldliness of contemporary evangelicalism. For criticism as well as appreciation of Wright's view, see Robert H. Gundry, "Reconstructing Jesus," *Christianity Today* 42/ 5 (April 27, 1998): 76-79 (with bibliographical references). The Jesus Seminar's hypothesis of a noneschatological historical Jesus who evolved into an eschatological but unhistorical Christ of faith reverses what sociologists of religion observe as the normal evolution of sects from futurism to presentism. From the sociological standpoint, then, this reverse evolution looks unlikely. Perhaps the economic theories of Gerhard E. Lenski and John H. Kautsky have afflicted the Jesus Seminar with a tunnel vision that neglects the theological evolution of sects.

49. I say "relatively" in acknowledgment of some ethical, social, and psychological implications in John's references to sins and evil deeds (but he never provides a list, as is often done elsewhere in the NT), to loving one another (but only in the Christian community, as noted above), and to an untroubled heart (but only in reference to Jesus' departure from and return to the disciples). Ethics may deal as much with the formation of character as with rules of behavior, but John does not relate even the new birth from above to character-formation.

not call North American evangelicals to break out of their provincialism and attend to voices from the church in the two-thirds world and from nonwhite, nonmiddleclass churches in their own backyard? Well and good, but we would probably learn from those sources precisely what John writes about, a sectarian separation from the world accompanied by a powerfully proclaimed Word from above. Or, as I have also been asked, why not call North American evangelicals to do their biblical and theological scholarship without embarrassment in the context of a worshiping community (cf. John 4:21-24), so that their scholarly agenda does not react to the interests of the academy so much as it responds to the needs of the church? Again well and good, but such a doxological and ecclesial turn strikes me as precisely sectarian rather than alternative to sectarianism.[50]

The Bible offers more than one theology of church and world — Luke-Acts represents almost the polar opposite of John's, for example (as a sidelight, contrast the typically institutional emphasis on sacraments in Luke-Acts with the typically sectarian deemphasis of sacraments in John,

---

50. Compare the development by Jonathan R. Wilson (*Living Faithfully,* 70-78) of Alasdair McIntyre's new kind of monasticism. Stanley Hauerwas and William H. Willimon (*Resident Aliens: Life in the Christian Colony* [Nashville: Abingdon, 1989], 39-48) adopt the typology of John Howard Yoder ("A People in the World: Theological Interpretation," in *The Concept of the Believer's Church* [ed. James Leo Garrett Jr.; Scottdale, Pa.: Herald Press, 1969], 252-83) in preference to H. Richard Niebuhr's; and they favor what Yoder calls the confessing church, which stands for a congregational worship of Christ in all things over against the individualism of conversionists and the secularism of activists: "It [the confessing church] seeks to influence the world by being the church," i.e. by presenting to the world a countercultural alternative community that conceives of conversion "as a long process of being baptismally engrafted into a new people . . . participating in secular movements against war, against hunger, and against other forms of inhumanity," and that sees this participation "as part of its necessary proclamatory action." There is something to be accepted in this position, but the stress on ethics and deeds for the improvement of present life differs markedly from John's stress on believing in the Word for the gaining of eternal life (cf. Harry J. Huebner, "Moral Agency as Embodiment: How the Church Acts," in *The Wisdom of the Cross: Essays in Honor of John Howard Yoder* [ed. Stanley Hauerwas et al.; Grand Rapids, Mich.: Eerdmans, 1999], 189-212).

not to detail Lukan cosmopolitanism) — and circumstances differ from place to place as well as from time to time. Judgments will differ accordingly, and for other reasons, too.[51] But the question is a serious one: Do our present circumstances call for John's Word-Christology, for North American evangelicalism to take a sectarian turn, a *return mutatis mutandis*, to the fundamentalism of *The Fundamentals* and their authors at the very start of the twentieth century?[52] Like that early fundamentalism and unlike the fundamentalism which evolved in the 20s-40s,[53] this new old fundamentalism, comparable in its neopaleoism to the new old commandment in 1 John 2:7-11; 3:11, would be culturally engaged with the world enough to be critical rather than so culturally secluded as to be mute, morally separate from the world but not spatially cloistered from it, and unashamedly expressive of historic Christian essentials but not quarrelsome over nonessentials.[54] Such a renewed fundamentalism

51. See, e.g., Joseph P. Huffman, "Faith, Reason, and the Text: The Return of the Middle Ages in Postmodern Scholarship," *Christian Scholar's Review* 29 (1999): 298: "Christians should be engaged in the quest ['for a transcendent and universal center'] rather than segregating themselves in academic and religious subcultures." Of course, John might tell Huffman that Christians have already found the transcendent and universal center and therefore do not need to join others in a quest for it, but need to disengage from the quest and announce its successful conclusion.

52. *The Fundamentals: A Testimony to the Truth* (4 vols.; Los Angeles: Bible Institute of Los Angeles, 1917). Oden (*After Modernity . . . What?* 66-69) does not like *The Fundamentals*, because they talk of historical events to the neglect of doctrine. But the proponents of *The Fundamentals* did interpret those historical events doctrinally (cf. Millard J. Erickson, *Postmodernizing the Faith: Evangelical Responses to the Challenge of Postmodernism* [Grand Rapids, Mich.: Baker, 1998], 61). It should be noted that the terms "fundamentalism" and "fundamentalist" came into vogue not till some time after publication of *The Fundamentals*.

53. But see some words of appreciation for mid-twentieth-century fundamentalism by Richard J. Mouw, *The Smell of Sawdust: What Evangelicals Can Learn from Their Fundamentalist Heritage* (Grand Rapids, Mich.: Zondervan, 2000).

54. It has been suggested to me that in some respects the original neoevangelicals (Carl F. H. Henry, Edward J. Carnell, Bernard Ramm, Ronald H. Nash et al.) resembled many of the original fundamentalists, the authors of *The Fundamentals* (W. H. Griffith Thomas, Melvin Grove Kyle, E. Y. Mullins, James Orr, George L. Robinson, Robert E. Speer, Benjamin B. Warfield, George Frederick

would take direction not only from fundamentalism at the very start of the twentieth century but also, and more importantly, from the paleo-fundamentalism of John the sectarian, whose Christology of the Word has Jesus come into the world (there is the engagement with it), sanctify himself (there is the separation from it[55]), and exegete God (there is the message to it).[56]

Wright et al.). With a return to the master narrative of Word-Christology, contrast the view of Robert Kysar, *Stumbling in the Light: New Testament Images for a Changing Church* (St. Louis: Chalice, 1999). Himself a Johannine scholar though not a conservative evangelical, Kysar thinks that in our culture of ambivalence and uncertainty the church should speak in new metaphors that are less self-assured and more tentative than the old ones of anchor, rock, and such like — as though the recent decline of some denominations in numbers and influence were due to dogmatism! Sociological analyses have discovered the opposite to be true.

55. Cf. John 8:46: "Which of you convicts me of sin?" So sanctified is Jesus in John that he is not said to have received baptism, associated as it is with repentance and confession of sin (see 1:29-36).

56. In speaking of the church at large, and probably more of nonevangelical than evangelical churches, Robert Kysar ("Coming Hermeneutical Earthquake in Johannine Interpretation," in *"What Is John?" Readers and Readings of the Fourth Gospel* [ed. Fernando F. Segovia; SBLSymS 3; Atlanta: Scholars Press, 1996], 185-86) predicts that in the twenty-first century Christians, having lost their dominance in society, will draw on John's Gospel "to understand themselves over against the world" and develop "a new other-worldliness." But Kysar worries whether they will "also be able to read and appropriate the Gospel's trans-sectarian motifs," by which he means inclusion of the socially marginalized, such as women and Samaritans. But sects commonly appeal to the socially marginalized, so that Kysar makes a mistake to treat John's inclusion of them as antithetical to sectarianism.

A Postscript on Some Theological Desiderata

As Christians should we bring to bear the totality of the Bible in our every situation so as to avoid imbalances and extremes? Or should we choose parts of the Bible that seem particularly relevant to a current situation and with a situational change shift to other parts so as to avoid the homogenizing of distinctive messages and a consequent loss of special applicability? Since the Bible is a collection of books (τὰ βιβλία) written under the inspiration of the Holy Spirit at different times and places by different authors in and for different circumstances, I have adopted here the situation-sensitive alternative. But these alternatives deserve full discussion. Doubtless some will argue for both/and rather than either/or. Others will propose further possibilities. But the basic questions remain: Does the Bible present theological data to be organized neatly, or a range of canonical options to be kept discrete? To what extent should the theological enterprise be systematic? To what extent selective? Ought systematic theology to dominate biblical theology, or vice versa? Or ought they form a partnership of equals, or go their separate ways? What weight should be assigned to theological common ground in the Bible? What weight to theological peculiarities? How important to good theologizing is a perceptive exegesis of the world, or worlds, in which we live as well as a perceptive exegesis of the Bible? And in practice, if not expressly, what answers to these questions has recent evangelical theology given?

Extended Endnotes

The Transfiguration of Jesus according to John: Jesus as the Heard Word

It is not my present purpose to discuss in detail the origin of John's Word-Christology, or to offer a full explanation of its origin. But following is a suggestion that may provide at least a partial explanation. John's portrayal of Jesus as the Word who according to Peter has "the words of eternal life" (6:68) and who says, "The one hearing my word and believing him who sent me has eternal life" (5:24), recalls the voice of God that came to Peter, James, and John at the transfiguration, "Hear him" (Mark 9:7 par. Matt 17:5 par. Luke 9:35). This voice also pronounced Jesus to be God's "beloved Son," just as John repeatedly portrays Jesus as the Son of God and as such the supreme object of God's love (1:34, 49; 3:16, 17, 18, 35, 36 [*bis*]; 5:19 [*bis*], 20, 21, 22, 23 [*bis*], 25, 26; 6:40; 8:36; 10:17, 36; 11:4, 27; 14:13, 23; 15:9, 10; 17:1 [*bis*], 23, 24, 26; 19:7; 20:31). Furthermore, John portrays this supreme object of God's love as the "only" (μονογενής) Son of God, just as at the close of the transfiguration the disciples see Jesus "only" (μόνον). Earlier, the divine voice had come "out of the cloud," just as in John 12:28-29 the voice of the Father came "out of the sky/heaven," so that some were saying "it had thundered." According to Matt 17:2 Jesus' face shone "like the sun and his garments became

97

white as the light." So also in John, Jesus the Word is "the light of the world" (8:12; 9:5), metaphorically equivalent to the sun (11:9; see also 3:19 [*bis*], 20, 21; 12:35, 36, 46 and esp. 1:4, 5, 7, 8, 9 for an association of the Word with light; cf. Rev 1:16). This Word who is the light has "glory," and people "beheld his glory" (1:14; 2:11; 8:54; 12:41; 17:5, 22, 24), just as according to Luke 9:32 "Peter and the ones with him . . . saw his [Jesus'] glory." The three tents suggested by Peter but rejected by God at the transfiguration reduce to one divinely sanctioned tent in John 1:14: "And the Word [who is 'the only God' — 1:18] became flesh and tented among us," so that "grace and truth came through Jesus Christ" in contrast with the giving of "the law through Moses" (1:16), who along with Elijah at the transfiguration talked with Jesus about "his exodus . . . in Jerusalem" (Luke 9:31), where according to John 19:33-36 Jesus died as the true Passover in recollection of the first Passover at the exodus in Moses' time. Under the view that John knew and used the synoptics, or that he used tradition that made its way into the synoptics, it looks as though John may have developed his Word-Christology, and much else related to it, out of the transfiguration of Jesus.

In Defense of "Exegesis" in John 1:18

The text-critical questions in John 1:18 need not detain us (one variant reading puts the definite article before "unique one," and another variant reading additionally has "Son" instead of "God"), but the verb ἐξηγήσατο demands our attention. Ignace de la Potterie ("'C'est lui qui a ouvert la voie': La finale du prologue johannique," *Bib* 69 [1988]: 340-70; cf. idem, *La vérité,* 1:213-28; also M. E. Boismard, *St. John's Prologue* [London: Blackfriars, 1957], 67, 70; Luc Devillers, "Exégèse et théologie de Jean I, 18," *Revue Thomiste* 89 [1989]: 181-217) has argued that the semantic associations of this verb in John differ from those of the same verb when it is used elsewhere in the sense of exegesis, and that for lack of an expressed accusative of direct object and for lack elsewhere of a personal object where the verb has to do with exegesis, here the verb does not have to do with exegesis; rather, with leading or showing the way. Thus, after coming out of the Father's bosom and by returning into the Father's bosom, Jesus has opened the way for us and leads us with himself into the Father's bosom (cf. 14:6).

But Potterie's own discussion puts on display a variety of semantic associations where ἐξηγέομαι has the sense of exegesis, so that the difference of those associations in John does not demand a different sense for the verb. In the Greek language, moreover, objects often have to be supplied from the context; John's omission of an object lets all the stress fall on exegesis as such (Hartmut Gese, *Essays on Biblical Theology* [trans. Keith Crim; Minneapolis: Augsburg, 1981], 186; Michael Theobald, *Die Fleischwerdung des Logos: Studien zum Verhältnis des Johannesprologs zum Corpus des Evangeliums und zu 1 Joh* [NTAbh NS 20; Münster: Aschendorff, 1988], 261-62); and even Potterie's interpretation requires an ellipsis, viz., either the ellipsis of a genitive object for the ones *of* whom the unique one is the leader or the ellipsis of a dative object for the ones *to* whom a way is shown (LSJ s.v. ἐξηγέομαι I 3-4). The expression of a personal object in the accusative might have left a misimpression that the verb has to do with governing. As it is, several factors favor that ἐξηγήσατο means "has exegeted" with "the Father," just mentioned, to be inferred as the object of exegesis: (1) nobody's ever having seen God in the first part of 1:18; (2) the preceding identification of the unique one as "the Word"; and (3) the special use of ἐξηγέομαι for priests', soothsayers', and deities' imparting information about divine secrets (Harris, *Prologue and Gospel*, 109-15; C. Spicq, "ἐξηγέομαι," *TLNT* 2:21-23).

It is another question whether to gain a typically Johannine double entendre we should add the meaning of leadership into the Father's bosom (see Robert, "La double intention," 435-41; idem, "Le mot final du prologue johannique: A propos d'un article récent," *Revue Thomiste* 89 [1989]: 279-88; idem, "Un précédent platonicien à l'équivoque de Jean 1, 18," *Revue Thomiste* 90 [1990]: 634-39; Walther Bindemann, "Der Johannesprolog: Ein Versuch, ihn zu verstehen," *NovT* 37 [1995]: 330-54). But several considerations militate against construing εἰς τὸν κόλπον τοῦ πατρός with ἐκεῖνος ἐξηγήσατο ("that one has led [us] into the bosom of the Father") — as a result of which construal ὁ ὤν, "the one existing," stands absolute in allusion to Exod 3:14 LXX and in anticipation of Jesus' ἐγὼ εἰμί, "I am," later in John — rather than traditionally with ὁ ὤν ("the one existing in the bosom of the Father"): (1) In the non-traditional construal, εἰς and ἐξ- conflict with each other; you would expect εἰσηγήσατο rather than ἐξηγήσατο to go with εἰς τὸν κόλπον τοῦ πατρός. (2) ἐκεῖνος is interruptive; you would expect it to precede rather than follow the εἰς-phrase, which by telling where is adverbial. For in 1:33; 2:21; 5:11, 37; 8:44; 12:48; 13:25, 30; 15:26; 20:15, 16 ἐκεῖνος precedes an adverbial expression connected with the verb for which ἐκεῖνος acts as a subject. The only exceptions appear in 5:46; 7:45; 9:12; 20:13; and, not as in 1:18, none of these exceptions offer a possibility of taking the adverbial expression with a preceding verbal expression. (3) The sense of direction in εἰς with the verb of being in 1:18 corresponds to the sense of direction in πρός with the verb of being in 1:1, where the πρός-phrase describes the relation to God the Father of the Word who was God, whereas to take the εἰς-phrase in 1:18 with ἐξήγησατο would divorce that phrase from the Word and thus spoil the parallelistic *inclusio* with 1:1.

The unusualness of exegeting a person should not bother us; John regularly uses language in unusual ways (see the whole of Petersen's *Sociology of Light*). Right within the Prologue, for example, John's side-by-side distinguishing of the Word from God and equating of the Word with God provide an obvious example. Jesus' later statement, "The one having seen me has seen the Father" (14:9), provides another example of unusual language, and that example links nicely with Jesus as the one who exegetes the Father. Furthermore, ἐξηγέομαι does appear elsewhere in the sense of exegeting a person (Plato, *Cratylus* 407b: ἐξηγούμενοι τὸν ποιητόν, "exegeting the poet [viz., Homer]"). See further Gunnar H. Østenstad, *Patterns of Redemption in the Fourth Gospel: An Experiment in Structural Analysis* (Studies in the Bible and Early Christianity 38; Lewiston, N.Y.: Mellen, 1998), 85-93, 290-91; also Obermann, *Die christologische Erfüllung*, 338-40. Obermann notes that Jesus' being the way to the Father in 14:6 lies much more distant from 1:18 than does Jesus' being the Word in 1:1-17.

Angelomorphic Christology in Revelation 10:
A Backup for the Same in John 1:51

It is disappointing that Peter R. Carrell (*Jesus and the Angels: Angelology and the Christology of the Apocalypse of John* [SNTSMS 95; Cambridge: Cambridge University Press, 1997], 131-38), though accepting angelomorphic Christology elsewhere in the Apocalypse, rejects an identification of the angel in ch. 10 with Jesus. According to Carrell, "Gundry . . . overlooks the point that against the wider context of glorious angels, the angel in Apc. 10.1 is not unusual and thus there is no need to press the resemblance to the conclusion that the angel is Jesus" (p. 137n.36). Astonishingly, however, Carrell overlooks that this angel has an opened scroll in his hand; that in ch. 5 Jesus the Lamb took a seven-sealed scroll from the hand of God; that between chs. 5 and 10 Jesus has loosened all the seals of the scroll so as to open it; that the interchange between opening it, loosening its seals, and opening its seals in 5:2, 4-5, 9; 6:1, 3, 5, 7, 9, 12; 8:1 equates the loosening of the seals with the opening of the scroll; that the vocalic reduplication of the perfect participle ἠνεῳγμένον no fewer than three times — first with η, second with ε, and third with ω — and the repetition of this participial form in 10:2, 8 make it hard to miss an emphasis on Jesus' having opened the scroll as a consequence of loosening its seals; that the interchange between βιβλίον and βιβλαρίδιον in 10:2, 8, 9, 10 (cf. the interchange of βίβλος and βιβλίον elsewhere in the Apocalypse, for which see 3:5; 13:8; 17:8; 20:12; 21:27) subverts any argument from βιβλαρίδιον that the scroll in ch. 10 differs from the one in ch. 5, where only βιβλίον occurs; that according to ch. 5 only Jesus is worthy to take and open the scroll by loosening-opening its seals; that the events which took place during the course of Jesus' opening the seals of the scroll have led to his taking possession of the world, as represented not only by the opened state of the scroll but also by the planting of the angel's feet on sea and land (so that the scroll is to be seen as a title deed to the world; for the planting of one's feet on something as taking possession of it, see Gen 13:17; Deut 1:36; 11:25; Josh 1:1-9; 4:9; Zech 14:4; Acts 7:5); that the reversal of the usual order of land first and then sea (5:13; 7:1-3; 12:12; 14:7) stresses a subjugation of the powers of chaos, represented by the sea, as only Jesus can accomplish; that the mention of standing on sea and land no fewer than three times in ch. 10 adds to this stress; and that the comparison of the angel's feet to pillars of fire recalls the divine theophany that led Israel in the wilderness (cf. the Exodus-theme that runs throughout the Apocalypse).

Also against Carrell, the angel's being "clothed" with a cloud does not describe a mode of transport so much as it tells something about the angel himself; it makes for a theophany insofar as the Apocalypse portrays Jesus, here in angelic form, as divine (cf. the angel of Yahweh in the OT). That 10:1 uses a different word for "face" (πρόσωπον) from the one for Jesus' face in 1:16 (ὄψις) poses no problem for angelomorphic Christology in ch. 10; for John the Seer often uses synonyms without distinction in meaning (see, e.g., μαστοί and στήθη for breasts in 1:13 and 15:6; "the ruler [ἄρχων] of the kings of the earth" and "the King of kings" in 1:5; 17:14; 19:16; "the alpha and the omega," "the first and the last," and "the beginning and the end" in 1:8, 17; 2:8; 21:6; 22:13; "white garments," "white robes," "washed robes," "clean white linen," and "clean bright linen" in 3:5, 18; 4:4; 6:11; 7:9, 13, 14; 19:8, 14; 22:14; "the Devil," "Satan," "the serpent," and "the dragon" in 2:9, 10; 12:3, 4, 7, 9, 12-17; 13:2, 4, 11; 20:2, 7, 10; and "forty-two months" and "1,260 days" in 11:2, 3; 12:6; 13:5; cf. the well-known penchant for synonyms in the Gospel of John); and the comparison of both Jesus' face and the angel's face to the sun favors an identification of the angel with Jesus. As to John's falling at Jesus' feet in 1:17 but not at the angel's feet in ch. 10, John finds himself already within arm's length of Jesus at 1:17 ("and he put his right hand on me"), so that proximity makes natural a knee-jerk reaction (pun intended), whereas in ch. 10 John sees a cosmic figure astride sea and land at a distance, so that John has to "go" (ὕπαγε — v. 8), i.e. "go away" (ἀπῆλθα — v. 9; note again the use of synonyms), to take the opened scroll out of the angel's hand.

The use in ch. 10 of βιβλίον as well as βιβλαρίδιον for a scroll small enough to be eaten by John shows that here βιβλίον is not to be taken as a faded diminutive; so there is no need to consider βιβλίον in ch. 5 as a faded diminutive referring to a larger scroll (cf. the use of βιβλίον in Deut 24:1, 3 LXX; Matt 19:7 for a bill of divorce with the dimensions of the bill of divorce discovered among the Dead Sea Scrolls, 112 x 220 mm. [Mur 19]; see also Herodotus, *Hist.* 1.123-24, for a βιβλίον so small as to allow concealment in the belly of a hare and to contain material that occupies only half a page of Greek text in the Loeb edition, which features tiny pages to begin with; ibid., 3.128, for many βιβλία the contents of which consist of only a single statement each). The anarthrousness of the opened scroll in 10:2 is due to the scroll's having been unopened as yet in ch. 5, not to the introduction of a different scroll in ch. 10.

The treatment of Revelation 10 by Loren T. Stuckenbruck (*Angel Veneration and Christology: A Study in Early Judaism and in the Christology of the Apocalypse of John* [WUNT 2/70; Tübingen: Mohr (Siebeck), 1995], 229-32) shares many of the deficiencies of Carrell's. For further details, see pp. 663-69 of my article, "Angelomorphic Christology in the Book of Revelation," and for general background, William Horbury, *Jewish Messianism and the Cult of Christ* (London: SCM, 1998), 119-217.

Tension with the World as a
Distinguishing Feature of Sectarianism

Although sociologists often disagree among themselves on the characteristics of sects, by and large they concur that tension with the world, or antiworldliness, constitutes the most consistently distinguishing feature, indeed a sine qua non, of sectarianism. See above all Johnson, "On Church and Sect," 539-49 ("the distinction between church and sect involves a single variable the values of which range along a continuum from complete rejection to complete acceptance of the environment" [p. 543]); idem, "Church and Sect Revisited," 124-37 ("There is little agreement on how the [church-sect] typology should be defined, but most sociologists do agree that a religious body's attitude toward its social environment should be a part of the definition" [p. 124]); also Weber, *Protestant Ethic,* 144-54; idem, *The Sociology of Religion* (trans. Ephraim Fischoff; Boston: Beacon, 1963), 144-54, 270-74; Troeltsch, *Social Teaching,* 1:331-43; Peter L. Berger, "Sociological Study of Sectarianism," 477-81; Russell R. Dynes, "The Consequences of Sectarianism for Social Participation," *Social Forces* 35 (1956-57): 331-34; Bryan R. Wilson, *Patterns of Sectarianism: Organisation and Ideology in Social and Religious Movements* (London: Heinemann, 1967), 36-37; idem, *Religious Sects* (New York: McGraw-Hill, 1970), 36-47; idem, *Social Dimensions of Sectarianism*, 46-68; Ammerman, *Bible Believers*, 72-102; Johnstone, *Religion in Society*, 93.

On the refinement of church-sect typology, see Johnstone, *Religion in Society*, 109-10; Rodney Stark, "Church and Sect," in *The Sacred in a Secular Age: Toward Revision in the Scientific Study of Religion* (ed. Phillip E. Hammond; Berkeley: University of California Press, 1985), 139-49; Winter, *Continuities*, 109-16; Roberts, *Religion in Sociological Perspective*, 223-39.

For criticisms of church-sect typology, see Erich Goode, "Some Critical Observations on the Church-Sect Dimension," *Journal for the Scientific Study of Religion* 6 (1967): 69-77; Nicholas J. Demerath III, "In a Sow's Ear: A Reply to Goode," *Journal for the Scientific Study of Religion* 6 (1967): 77-84; idem, "Son of a Sow's Ear," *Journal for the Scientific Study of Religion* 6 (1967): 275-77; Allan W. Eister, "Toward a Radical Critique of Church-Sect Typologizing: Comment on 'Some Critical Observations on the Church-Sect Dimension,'" *Journal for the Scientific Study of Religion* 6 (1967): 85-99; Bengt Holmberg, *Sociology and the New Testament: An Appraisal* (Minneapolis: Fortress, 1990), 108-14.

The criticisms by J. Kenneth Benson and James H. Dorsett ("Toward a Theory of Religious Organizations," *Journal for the Scientific Study of Religion* 10 [1971]: 138-51) leave out of account the theological views of sectarians in reference to the religious establishment and the world. James A. Beckford ("Religious Organization," *Current Sociology* 21 [1973]: 92-104) calls for a moratorium on church-sect typology, but his criticisms seem to rest mainly on an inability of that typology to say very much about the organizational structures of religion, the topic in which he is most interested. James E. Dittes ("Typing the Typologies: Some Parallels in the Career of Church-Sect and Extrinsic-Intrinsic," *Journal for the Scientific Study of Religion* 10 [1971]: 375-83) criticizes the axiological use of church-sect typology, but ends his article with an admission that the persistence with which sociologists find the typology useful means that "they must be doing something right, or at least congenial to many social scientists [i.e. to their own religious predispositions]." Lawson ("Sects and Churches," 16-18) notes sociologists' recent return "to the church-sect problem complex, armed with better empirical data."

The Restriction of Love to Fellow Believers in First John

John A. T. Robinson (*Priority*, 332-33) mounts several arguments against a restriction of love to fellow believers in 1 John:

1. The point in 1 John 4:20 lies in a contrast between the visibility of a "neighbor" and the invisibility of God. Yes to the contrast between visibility and invisibility; but Robinson illegitimately substitutes "neighbor" for 1 John's "brother." The visibility of an unbelieving neighbor is therefore irrelevant to the point being made.
2. "Sheer humanity" is at issue in 1 John 3:16-17. No, brotherhood is at issue; for the passage uses only the language of brotherhood.
3. Since in 1 John 2:9-11 the gnosticizers who hate their brothers contrast with believers who love their brothers, the believers' love must cross the boundaries of 1 John's community just as the gnosticizers' hatred crosses the boundaries of the gnostic community. But 1 John is using the language of Christian profession, which profession the author regards as false in the case of the haters, as true in the case of the hated. The generality of human beings is not in view (cf. Brooke Foss Westcott, *The Epistles of St John: The Greek Text with Notes* [3d ed.; Grand Rapids, Mich.: Eerdmans, 1966], 55: "There is, as far as it appears, no case where a fellow-man, as man, is called 'a brother' in the N.T.").
4. It would not make sense to disapprove of the world's hatred toward believers in 1 John 3:13-14 yet limit the love of believers to each other (cf. Rudolf Schnackenburg, *The Moral Teaching of the New Testament* [trans. J. Holland-Smith and W. J. O'Hara; New York: Herder, 1965], 328). But mutual love among believers provides a refuge from the world's hatred of them. Therefore a love of believers for the world need not come into the picture at all — and should

not, in view of 2:15-17. Moreover, 1 John does not tell believers to hate the world, so that a limitation of love to fellow believers does not make nonsensical the disapproval of the world's hatred of them.

Robinson is trying to refute H. Montefiore, "Thou Shalt Love Thy Neighbor as Thyself," *NovT* 5 (1962): 157-70, esp. 164-65. In respect to each of Robinson's arguments, we should note that Hellenistic papyri and inscriptions use "brothers" for members of the same religious association (Klauck, "Brudermord and Bruderliebe," 166n.40). All in all, then, the restriction of love to fellow believers in 1 John links up with the same, and with only God's loving the world, in the Gospel of John.

God loves the world with the purpose of drawing out of it and to his Son some of those unbelievers who make up the world, so that they no longer belong to it but enter the circle of believers' love for one another. Could it be, then, that the command in 1 John not to love the world was occasioned by circumstances in which loving the world, i.e. worldlings, would have bred among believers such worldliness, i.e. the lust of the flesh, the lust of the eyes, and the pride of livelihood, that their love for one another would have been lost and consequently its evangelistic attractiveness? If so, we need to elucidate what those circumstances were and ask whether our current circumstances match them.

Questions about the Sociological Causes of John's Alienation from the World and about Anti-Semitism in John

As to the sociological causes of John's alienation from the world, one can think of expulsion from the synagogue (cf. 9:22, 34; 12:42; 16:2), embracement of the world by "gnostic" secessionists (cf. 1 John 2:19, though many would date the secession later than John's Gospel — yet see John 6:60-71), and the magnificence of idolatry in Ephesus (if John wrote there). One can also think in reverse that the social rejection of John's community arose out of their turning against the world. Most likely is a symbiotic relation between the community's rejecting the world and the world's rejecting them (cf. Dokka, "Irony and Sectarianism," 100; Nissen, "Community and Ethics," 196-98).

Inasmuch as "the world" that John excoriates includes Gentiles as well as Jews (see esp. 4:22 with 4:9; cf. Harnack, "Ueber das Verhältnis," 192; Nissen, "Community and Ethics," 208-10), I prescind from discussing in detail the question of anti-Semitism in John's use of "the Jews," though it should be noted in passing that in 4:9 Jesus accepts the description of him as "a Jew"; that in 4:22 he declares, "We [Jews] know what we worship, because salvation is of the Jews"; and that in 11:45; 12:9-19 "many of the Jews" believed in Jesus (cf. 8:31, though there the following verses call in question the genuineness of belief). Against limiting "the Jews" to Judeans (so Malina and Rohrbaugh, *Social-Science Commentary on the Gospel of John*, 44-46 et passim, and others before them) are again Jesus' accepting the description of him as a Jew (contrast his retort in 8:48 to being called a Samaritan — a contrast unnoted by Malina and Rohrbaugh [ibid., 99], who think that the Samaritan woman tagged Jesus as an outsider by calling him a Judean, just as the Judeans tagged him as an outsider by calling him a Samaritan); also the inclusion of Jesus in the "we" who are "the Jews" from whom salvation comes. Since God sent him "in order that the world might be saved through him" (3:17), for salvation to come from the Jews Jesus must have been a Jew though he was a Galilean, not a Judean (7:52). And how could Judeans, who did not receive him, be "his own" if he, a Galilean, was not one of them (1:11)? See also 18:35, where Pilate says, "I am not a Jew, am I? *Your* nation [made up of the Jews] and the chief priests [their leaders] gave you over to me" (italics added).

For more details see Thomas Söding, "'Was kann aus Nazareth schon Gutes kommen?' (Joh 1.46): Die Bedeutung des Judeseins Jesu im Johannesevangelium," *NTS* 46 (2000): 21-41; and for an evaluative survey of different views on John's use of "the Jews," Urban C. von Wahlde, "'The Jews' in the Gospel of John: Fifteen Years of Research (1983-1998)," *ETL* 76 (2000): 30-55, and esp. 37, 47-51 on the translation "the Judeans." Von Wahlde concludes, "There is absolutely no reason to think that the hostility evident in passages where 'the Jews' appear is based on political or ethnic considerations. This is all but universally agreed to. The issue throughout is competing assessments of the meaning and identity of Jesus in relation to the religious claims of the Israelite tradition" (cf. G. Van Belle, "International Interdisciplinary Seminar on the Fourth Gospel," *ETL* 76 [2000]: 216-18; *Anti-Judaism and the Fourth Gospel: Papers of the Leuven Colloquium, 2000* [ed. R. Bieringer, D. Pollefeyt, and F. Vandecasteele-Vanneuville; Jewish and Christian Heritage Series 1; Assen: Van Gorcum, 2001]).

Exclusivism, Inclusivism, and Universalism in Relation to John's Gospel

The increasing popularity of inclusivism among evangelicals is due partly to their near canonization of C. S. Lewis's writings and to the resultant influence, in particular, of the inclusivistic scene in ch. 15 of *The Last Battle* (New York: Macmillan, 1956), where the christic lion Aslan welcomes and takes to himself the services rendered by the heathen Emeth to the satanic Tash, because — benighted though Emeth has been — he has all along been seeking the truth (pp. 155-57). It remains to be seen what effect on Christian evangelism and missionary endeavor the migration from exclusivism through inclusivism toward universalism will have, but Burdick and Hammond ("World Order and Mainline Religions," 198-205) chart a decline in past American foreign missions with the shift of purpose in three stages: (1) from the conversion of non-Christians (2) through the exercise of philanthropic compassion on them (3) to a co-religious companionship with them. And it seems likely that the passion for souls that carries over from many inclusivists' upbringing in exclusivistic circles will dissipate among second and third generation inclusivists. Bringing people to Christ merely sooner than they otherwise would come to him does not provide so strong a motivation for evangelism and missions as does the bringing of people to Christ who would otherwise be forever lost. The extensive sociological fieldwork conducted by Christian Smith and his colleagues during the years 1995-97 (Christian Smith, *Christian America? What Evangelicals Really Want* [Berkeley: University of California Press, 2000], 81-87) shows that though evangelicals on the whole do not beat non-Christians over the head with threats of hellfire and brimstone, the belief in eternal damnation for those who do not come to Christ during their earthly lifetimes does provide a motivation for Christian witness, plus a sense of guilt for not engaging in evangelism more avidly.

As to universalism, in a doctoral seminar at Basel, Switzerland, during the academic year 1960-61 I remember Karl Barth's saying in answer to the question why he did not affirm universalism even though it seemed to follow from the rest of his soteriology, "If I were forced to take a position, I would affirm universalism; but I do not affirm it, because affirming it would cut the nerve of Christian evangelism" (or words to that effect). I take his statement not as rhetorically tactical ("In my heart of hearts I believe in universalism but will not say so lest Christian evangelism be inhibited") but as theologically fundamental ("There must be something wrong with any doctrine that inhibits Christian evangelism").

With Barth's drawing back, contrast the forward push of Barclay ("Universalism and Particularism," 222-23):

> But its [Christendom's] new status in the post-Christian West requires it to reassemble artificial boundaries [as opposed to 'many natural boundaries' that Christianity acquired during its ascendancy in the West, i.e. natural boundaries of 'family, social class, country, even continent and empire'] like those it employed in its first centuries. Thus, there now re-emerges the danger of a self-enclosed sectarian spirit which lurks in the New Testament vision of the Church. Perhaps what is required of Christians now is an honest renunciation of Christian particularity . . . , a renunciation of past imperialist ambitions, a commitment to exploit the world-affirming aspects of the Christian tradition, and a liberality which recognizes the complementary contributions to human welfare which are made by those outside the Christian community. . . . the recognition . . . also encourages a Christian universalism which applauds and supports the work of divine grace wherever it is manifested.

It is hard to imagine a more anti-Johannine sentiment.

For inclusivism, see Amos Young, "Whither Inclusivism? The Development and Critique of an Evangelical Theology of Religions," *EvQ*

71 (1999): 327-48; John Sanders, *No Other Name: An Investigation into the Destiny of the Unevangelized* (Grand Rapids, Mich.: Eerdmans, 1992); Paul Lakeland, *Postmodernity: Christian Identity in a Fragmented Age* (Guides to Theological Inquiry; Minneapolis: Fortress, 1997), 76-113; Daniel Strange, "Clark H. Pinnock: The Evolution of an Evangelical Maverick," *EvQ* 7 (1999): 311-26; Clark H. Pinnock, *A Wideness in God's Mercy: The Finality of Jesus Christ in a World of Religions* (Grand Rapids, Mich.: Zondervan, 1992); idem, *Flame of Love: A Theology of the Holy Spirit* (Downers Grove, Ill.: InterVarsity Press, 1996), 185-214. Against inclusivism, see Erickson, *Evangelical Left,* 109-23, 127-30; Carson, *Gagging of God,* 278-314; John Piper, *Let the Nations Be Glad! The Supremacy of God in Missions* (Grand Rapids, Mich.: Baker, 1993), 115-66, 221-22. For various views, see *Four Views of Salvation in a Pluralistic World* (ed. Dennis L. Okholm and Timothy R. Phillips; Grand Rapids, Mich.: Zondervan, 1995); Grenz, *Renewing the Center,* 249-68, with a wide bibliography.

The Sectarian Start of Christianity

According to N. J. Demerath III and Phillip E. Hammond (*Religion in Social Context* [New York: Random House, 1969], 74), "there is little disagreement that the early Christian movement conformed closely to the sect model." On Jesus' attempt to reform Judaism see Klaus Berger, *Theologiegeschichte,* 93-94 (in connection with dualism, which sociologists regard as often characteristic of sectarianism); Christopher Rowland, *Christian Origins: From Messianic Movement to Christian Religion* (Minneapolis: Augsburg, 1985), 111-17, 133-36; Howard Clark Kee, *Knowing the Truth: A Sociological Approach to the New Testament* (Minneapolis: Fortress, 1989), 86-88; and, more extensively among others, Scot McKnight, *A New Vision for Israel: The Teachings of Jesus in National Context* (Grand Rapids, Mich.: Eerdmans, 1999); John P. Meier, *A Marginal Jew: Rethinking the Historical Jesus* (3 vols.; ABRL; New York: Doubleday, 1991-); E. P. Sanders, *The Historical Figure of Jesus* (London: Penguin, 1993); idem, *Jesus and Judaism* (Philadelphia: Fortress, 1985); N. T.

Wright, *The New Testament and the People of God* (Christian Origins and the Question of God 1; Minneapolis: Fortress, 1992); idem, *Jesus and the Victory of God* (Christian Origins and the Question of God 2; Minneapolis: Fortress, 1996). Amusingly, current scholarly recognition of Jesus' attempt to reform Judaism agrees with a major tenet of old-line dispensationalism in fundamentalist circles, i.e. Jesus' offer of the kingdom to Israel on condition of their repentance and acceptance of him.

Jack T. Sanders (*Schismatics,* 114-25) resists describing primitive Christianity as sectarian, because it did not secede from Judaism. But though it had not yet broken away from Judaism, or been driven away, during Jesus' lifetime, it had started as a typically sectarian protest. Many a sect begins as a protest or reformative movement within an institution (Werner Stark, *The Sociology of Religion: A Study of Christendom,* vol. 2: *Sectarian Religion* [New York: Fordham University Press, 1967], 128-29; Yinger, *Scientific Study of Religion,* 254-55); and despite continuing attendance at synagogue and temple, Christians' meeting regularly by themselves and bringing Gentile converts into their assemblies in large numbers should count as significantly secessionary. William Horbury (*Jews and Christians in Contact and Controversy* [Edinburgh: T&T Clark, 1998], 11-12) speaks of "a separative tendency" in Jesus' teaching "because of its implied claim to authority" and notes that "his followers already formed a recognizably Jewish group" and then had "separate meetings," though Jesus himself "looked . . . not for the foundation of a sect but for the renewal of Israel" (so also against Malina ["The Gospel of John in Sociolinguistic Perspective," 49-50], who underestimates the protestive, separatistic character of ancient sects in thinking that "to do sect analysis one needs free standing, non-embedded religion," such as did not exist in the first century).

Because primitive Christianity was already diverse, Barton too ("Early Christianity and the Sociology of the Sect," 141-45) resists describing it as sectarian; and Holmberg (*Sociology and the New Testament,* 90-91) argues that Judaism itself was so variegated that we cannot legitimately speak of it as a singular institution against which Christians could have reacted (see also L. Michael White, "Shifting Sectarian Boundaries in Early Christianity," *BJRL* 70 [1988]: 7-24). To be sure, there were differences within Judaism, and more than one sect. But Torah, temple, and synagogue provided a base broad enough to justify our speaking of an institutional Judaism that prompted the doing away with Jesus and the persecution of his followers thereafter, as in the case of Paul, who before his conversion persecuted Christians (Acts 8:3; 9:1-2, 13, 21; 22:4, 19; 26:10-11; 1 Cor 15:9; Gal 1:13-14; Phil 3:6; 1 Tim 1:13) and afterward suffered Jewish persecution himself (2 Cor 11:24, 26; 1 Thess 2:15, plus numerous passages in Acts; cf. the argument of Horbury, with support from the various works of E. P. Sanders, that "the Jewish community of the Second Temple period had stronger elements of order and cohesion than is usually allowed" [*Jews and Christians,* 1; see esp. 3-8, 43-110 against Ekkehard W. Stegemann and Wolfgang Stegemann, *The Jesus Movement: A Social History of Its First Century* (trans. O. C. Dean Jr.; Minneapolis: Fortress, 1999), 191-213, where the sectarian model is rejected in favor of the charismatic model as though sectarianism cannot be charismatic, whereas it is an observable fact that sectarianism is often charismatic, and a number of the characteristics that the brothers Stegemann detect in the Jesus movement correspond to sectarianism as described by modern sociologists]). Even under the view that because of Samaritan, Essene, and Therapeutic Judaisms, Second Temple Judaism has to be considered a sect alongside others (cf. White's view), one could well call the Jesus movement a sect that broke away from what had started as the sect of Second Temple Judaism and become a mainline institution. And whatever their differences Paul, James the Just, Peter, and John seem to have gotten along well enough for us to speak in the singular of Christianity (cf. Arland J. Hultgren, *The Rise of Normative Christianity* [Minneapolis: Augsburg Fortress, 1994]; Thomas A. Robinson, *The Bauer Thesis Examined: The Geography of Heresy in the Early Christian Church* [Lewiston, N.Y.: Edwin Mellen, 1988]).

Barton also argues that sociologists of religion have transposed the characteristics of primitive Christianity into the characteristics of a sect only to turn around and describe primitive Christianity as sectarian (cf. Holmberg, *Sociology and the New Testament,* 127-28, and the argument of Stanley Kent Stowers ["The Social Sciences and the Study of Early Christianity," in *Approaches to Ancient Judaism,* vol. 5: *Studies in Judaism and Its*

Greco-Roman Context (ed. William Scott Green; BJS 32; Atlanta: Scholars Press, 1985), 149-81] that modern social studies and ancient NT culture are incommensurable). The reverse, I think: sociologists of religion have mapped the characteristics of modern sects and noted that primitive Christianity exhibited many of those characteristics.

Barton is right, however, in calling attention to sociologists' tendency to underplay or ignore a determinative role of theological convictions — as distinct from circumstances of class, economy, gender, etc. — in the sociology of religion, including that of primitive Christianity. Cf. the denial by John Milbank (*Theology and Social Theory: Beyond Secular Reason* [Oxford: Blackwell, 1990]) that sociological descriptions equate with superior explanations of religious phenomena: "[the sociology of religion] cannot claim to be a true metadiscourse about religion, in contrast to theologies which merely represent world views. Such a claim only appears sustainable because sociology creates the illusion of a 'social fact'" (p. 110); "[we should reject] the implication that the 'social' aspects of Church life have some degree of causal determinacy over beliefs" (p. 120); "such a close unity [in the Johannine community] is not pre-given before the text, but rather is promoted by the text as an ethical and religious goal" (p. 121). These denials go too far, but they serve as healthy warnings against the sort of thing that one finds in Johnstone, *Religion in Society*, 92-96, to take but one example. Kieran Flanagan ("A Sociological Critique of Milbank," in *Theology and Sociology: A Reader* [ed. Robin Gill; 2d ed.; New York: Cassell, 1996], 451-60, esp. 457-58) points out that the reductive sociology which Milbank rails against does not characterize contemporary sociology as a whole.

Bibliography

Alford, Henry. *The Greek Testament: With a Critically Revised Text: A Digest of Various Readings: Marginal References to Verbal and Idiomatic Usage: Prolegomena and a Critical and Exegetical Commentary.* 4 vols., vol. 4 in two parts. 6th ed. London: Rivingtons, 1868.

Ammerman, Nancy Tatum. *Bible Believers: Fundamentalists in the Modern World.* New Brunswick, N.J.: Rutgers University Press, 1987.

Anderson, Paul N. *The Christology of the Fourth Gospel: Its Unity and Disunity in the Light of John 6.* Valley Forge, Pa.: Trinity Press International, 1996.

Anti-Judaism and the Fourth Gospel: Papers of the Leuven Colloquium, 2000. Edited by R. Bieringer, D. Pollefeyt, and F. Vandecasteele-Venneuville. Jewish and Christian Heritage Series 1. Assen: Van Gorcum, 2001.

Ashton, John. "The Transformation of Wisdom: A Study of the Prologue of John's Gospel." *New Testament Studies* 32 (1986): 161-186.

———. *Understanding the Fourth Gospel.* Oxford: Clarendon, 1991.

Bainbridge, William Sims. *The Sociology of Religious Movements.* New York: Routledge, 1997.

Ball, David Mark. *"I Am" in John's Gospel: Literary Function, Background, and Theological Implications.* Journal for the Study of the New Testament: Supplement Series 124. Sheffield: Sheffield Academic Press, 1996.

Balz, Horst, "Johanneische Theologie und Ethik im Licht der 'letzten Stunde.'" Pages 35-56 in *Studien zum Text und zur Ethik des Neuen Testaments.* Edited by Wolfgang Schrage. Berlin: Walter de Gruyter, 1986.

Barclay, John M. G. "Universalism and Particularism: Twin Components of Both Judaism and Early Christianity." Pages 207-224 in *A Vision for the*

115

Church: Studies in Early Christian Ecclesiology in Honour of J. P. M. Sweet. Edited by Markus Bockmuehl and Michael B. Thompson. Edinburgh: T&T Clark, 1997.

Barrett, C. K. *The Gospel according to St. John: An Introduction with Commentary and Notes on the Greek Text.* 2d ed. Philadelphia: Westminster, 1978.

————. "The Parallels between Acts and John." Pages 163-178 in *Exploring the Gospel of John.* Edited by R. Alan Culpepper and C. Clifton Black. Louisville, Ky.: Westminster John Knox, 1996.

Barton, Stephen C. "The Communal Dimension of Earliest Christianity." *Journal of Theological Studies* new series 43 (1992): 399-427.

————. "Early Christianity and the Sociology of the Sect." Pages 140-162 in *The Open Text: New Directions for Biblical Studies?* Edited by F. Watson. London: SCM, 1993.

————. "Historical Criticism and Social-Scientific Perspectives in New Testament Study." Pages 61-89 in *Hearing the New Testament.* Edited by Joel B. Green. Grand Rapids, Mich.: Eerdmans, 1995.

Beasley-Murray, George R. *Gospel of Life: Theology in the Fourth Gospel.* Peabody, Mass.: Hendrickson, 1991.

————. *John.* Word Biblical Commentary 36. Waco, Tex.: Word, 1987.

Beckford, James A. "Religious Organization." *Current Sociology* 21 (1973): 5-170.

Benson, J. Kenneth, and James H. Dorsett. "Toward a Theory of Religious Organizations." *Journal for the Scientific Study of Religion* 10 (1971): 138-151.

Berger, Klaus. *Exegese des Neuen Testaments: Neue Wege vom Text zur Auslegung.* 2d ed. Uni-Taschenbücher 658. Heidelberg: Quelle & Meyer, 1984.

————. *Im Anfang war Johannes: Datierung und Theologie des vierten Evangeliums.* Stuttgart: Quell, 1997.

————. *Theologiegeschichte des Urchristentums: Theologie des Neuen Testaments.* 2d ed. Tübingen: Francke, 1995.

Berger, Peter L. "A Call for Authority in the Christian Community: An Address Delivered to the 10th Plenary of the Consultation on Church Union, in Denver, Colorado." *The Christian Century* 88/43 (Oct. 27, 1971): 1257-1263.

————. "Religion and the American Future." Pages 65-77 in *The Third Century: America as a Post-Industrial Society.* Edited by Seymour Martin Lipset. Stanford, Calif.: Hoover Institution Press, 1979.

————. "The Sociological Study of Sectarianism." *Social Research* 21 (1954): 467-485.

Bindemann, Walther. "Der Johannesprolog: Ein Versuch, ihn zu verstehen." *Novum Testamentum* 37 (1995): 330-354.

Blank, Josef. *Das Evangelium Johannes.* 3 vols. Geistliche Schriftlesung. Düsseldorf: Patmos, 1981.

———. *Krisis: Untersuchungen zur johanneischen Christologie und Eschatologie.* Freiburg im Breisgau: Lambertus, 1964.

Boismard, M. E. "Jésus, le Prophète par excellence, d'après Jean 10. 24-39." Pages 160-171 in *Neues Testament und Kirche.* Edited by Joachim Gnilka. Freiburg: Herder, 1974.

———. *St. John's Prologue.* London: Blackfriars, 1957.

Braun, F.-M. *Jean le Théologien.* 3 vols., vol. 3 in two parts. Études bibliques. Paris: Gabalda, 1959-1972.

———. "La Réduction du Pluriel au Singulier dans l'Évangile et la Première Lettre de Jean." *New Testament Studies* 24 (1977-1978): 40-67.

Brodie, Thomas L. *The Gospel according to John: A Literary and Theological Commentary.* New York: Oxford University Press, 1993.

Brown, F., S. R. Driver, and C. A. Briggs. *A Hebrew and English Lexicon of the Old Testament.* Oxford: Clarendon, 1907.

Brown, Raymond E. *The Churches the Apostles Left Behind.* New York: Paulist, 1984.

———. *The Community of the Beloved Disciple.* New York: Paulist, 1979.

———. *The Death of the Messiah.* 2 vols. Anchor Bible Reference Library. New York: Doubleday, 1994.

———. *The Gospel according to John: Introduction, Translation, and Notes.* 2 vols. Anchor Bible 29-29A. Garden City, N.Y.: Doubleday, 1970.

Brueggemann, Walter. "II Kings 18–19: The Legitimacy of a Sectarian Hermeneutic." *Horizons in Biblical Theology* 7 (1985): 1-42.

Bultmann, Rudolf. *The Gospel of John: A Commentary.* Edited by R. W. N. Hoare and J. K. Riches. Translated by G. R. Beasley-Murray. Oxford: Blackwell, 1971.

———. *Theology of the New Testament.* Translated by Kendrick Grobel. 2 vols. New York: Scribner's, 1955.

Burdick, Michael A., and Phillip E. Hammond. "World Order and Mainline Religions: The Case of Protestant Foreign Missions." Pages 193-213 in *World Order and Religion.* Edited by Wade Clark Roof. SUNY Series in Religion, Culture, and Society. Albany, N.Y.: State University of New York Press, 1991.

Burge, Gary M. *The Anointed Community: The Holy Spirit in the Johannine Tradition.* Grand Rapids, Mich.: Eerdmans, 1987.

Buruma, Ian. "The Joys and Perils of Victimhood." *The New York Review of Books* 46/6 (April 8, 1999): 4, 6, 8-9.

Carpenter, Joel A. "From Fundamentalism to the New Evangelical Coalition." Pages 3-16 in *Evangelicalism and Modern America*. Edited by George Marsden. Grand Rapids, Mich.: Eerdmans, 1984.

————. *Revive Us Again: The Reawakening of American Fundamentalism*. New York: Oxford University Press, 1997.

Carrell, Peter R. *Jesus and the Angels: Angelology and the Christology of the Apocalypse of John*. Society of New Testament Studies Monograph Series 95. Cambridge: Cambridge University Press, 1997.

Carson, Donald A. *Divine Sovereignty and Human Responsibility: Biblical Perspectives in Tension*. New Foundations Theological Library. Atlanta: John Knox, 1980.

————. *The Gagging of God: Christianity Confronts Pluralism*. Grand Rapids, Mich.: Zondervan, 1996.

————. *The Gospel according to John*. Leicester, England: Inter-Varsity Press, 1991.

Cassem, N. H. "A Grammatical and Contextual Inventory of the Use of κόσμος in the Johannine Corpus with Some Implications for Cosmic Theology." *New Testament Studies* 19 (1972-1973): 81-91.

Chipp, Herschel B. *Theories of Modern Art: A Source Book by Artists and Critics*. Berkeley: University of California Press, 1968.

Clark, Gordon H. *The Johannine Logos*. Nutley, N.J.: Presbyterian and Reformed, 1972.

Corell, Alf. *Consummatum Est: Eschatology and Church in the Gospel of St. John*. London: SPCK, 1958.

Counet, Patrick Chatelion. *John, a Postmodern Gospel: Introduction to Deconstructive Exegesis Applied to the Fourth Gospel*. Biblical Interpretation Series 44. Leiden: Brill, 2000.

Cranfield, C. E. B. "John 1^{14}: 'became.'" *Expository Times* 93 (1981-1982): 215.

Culpepper, R. Alan. "The Gospel of John as a Document of Faith in a Pluralistic Culture." Pages 107-127 in *"What Is John?" Readers and Readings of the Fourth Gospel*. Edited by Fernando F. Segovia. Society of Biblical Literature Symposium Series 3. Atlanta: Scholars Press, 1996.

Dahl, Nils Alstrup. "Der Erstgeborene Satans und der Vater des Teufels (Polyk. 7 1 und Joh 8 44)." Pages 70-85 in *Apophoreta*. Beihefte zur Zeitschrift für die neutestamentliche Wissenschaft 30. Berlin: Töpelmann, 1964.

Davies, Margaret. *Rhetoric and Reference in the Fourth Gospel*. Journal for the

Study of the New Testament: Supplement Series 69. Sheffield: JSOT Press, 1992.

Demerath III, Nicholas J. "In a Sow's Ear: A Reply to Goode." *Journal for the Scientific Study of Religion* 6 (1967): 77-84.

———. "Son of a Sow's Ear." *Journal for the Scientific Study of Religion* 6 (1967): 275-277.

Demerath III, N. J., and Phillip E. Hammond. *Religion in Social Context.* New York: Random House, 1969.

Devillers, Luc. "Exégèse et théologie de Jean I, 18." *Revue Thomiste* 89 (1989): 181-217.

Dittes, James E. "Typing the Typologies: Some Parallels in the Career of Church-Sect and Extrinsic-Intrinsic." *Journal for the Scientific Study of Religion* 10 (1971): 375-383.

Dodd, C. H. *How to Read the Gospels.* Westminster, U.K.: Church Information Board, 1956.

———. *The Interpretation of the Fourth Gospel.* Cambridge: Cambridge University Press, 1960.

Dokka, Trond Skard. "Irony and Sectarianism in the Gospel of John." Pages 83-107 in *New Readings in John: Literary and Theological Perspectives: Essays from the Scandinavian Conference on the Fourth Gospel, Aarhus 1997.* Edited by Johannes Nissen and Sigfred Pedersen. Journal for the Study of the New Testament: Supplement Series 182. Sheffield: Sheffield Academic Press, 1999.

Drury, John. *Painting the Word: Christian Pictures and Their Meanings.* New Haven, Conn.: Yale University Press, 1999.

Dunderberg, Ismo. "Johannine Anomalies and the Synoptics." Pages 108-125 in *New Readings in John: Literary and Theological Perspectives: Essays from the Scandinavian Conference on the Fourth Gospel, Aarhus 1997.* Edited by Johannes Nissen and Sigfred Pedersen. Journal for the Study of the New Testament: Supplement Series 182. Sheffield: Sheffield Academic Press, 1999.

Dunn, James D. G. "Let John Be John: A Gospel for Its Time." Pages 309-340 in *The Gospel and the Gospels.* Edited by P. Stuhlmacher. Grand Rapids, Mich.: Eerdmans, 1991.

Dunn, James M. "Fundamentalism and the American Polity: A Response." Pages 143-150 in *The Fundamentalist Phenomenon: A View from Within; A Response from Without.* Edited by Norman J. Cohen. Starkoff Institute Studies in Ethics and Contemporary Moral Problems. Grand Rapids, Mich.: Eerdmans, 1990.

Dynes, Russell R. "Church-Sect Typology and Socio-Economic Status." *American Sociological Review* 20 (1955): 555-560.

———. "The Consequences of Sectarianism for Social Participation." *Social Forces* 35 (1956-1957): 331-334.

Eister, Allan W. "Toward a Radical Critique of Church-Sect Typologizing: Comment on 'Some Critical Observations on the Church-Sect Dimension.'" *Journal for the Scientific Study of Religion* 6 (1967): 85-90.

Ellis, E. Earle. "New Testament Teaching on Hell." Pages 199-219 in *Eschatology in Bible and Theology: Evangelical Essays at the Dawn of a New Millennium.* Edited by Kent E. Brower and Mark W. Elliott. Downers Grove, Ill.: InterVarsity, 1997.

Erickson, Millard J. *The Evangelical Left: Encountering Postconservative Evangelical Theology.* Grand Rapids, Mich.: Baker, 1997.

———. *Postmodernizing the Faith: Evangelical Responses to the Challenge of Postmodernism.* Grand Rapids, Mich.: Baker, 1998.

Esler, Philip F. *The First Christians in Their Social Worlds: Social-Scientific Approaches to New Testament Interpretation.* London: Routledge, 1994.

Finke, Roger, and Rodney Stark. *The Churching of America, 1776-1990: Winners and Losers in Our Religious Economy.* New Brunswick, N.J.: Rutgers University Press, 1992.

Flanagan, Kieran. "A Sociological Critique of Milbank." Pages 451-460 in *Theology and Sociology: A Reader.* Edited by Robin Gill. 2d ed. New York: Cassell, 1996.

Fossum, Jarl E. *The Image of the Invisible God: Essays on the Influence of Jewish Mysticism on Early Christology.* Novum Testamentum et Orbis Antiquus 30. Göttingen: Vandenhoeck & Ruprecht, 1995.

Four Views of Salvation in a Pluralistic World. Edited by Dennis L. Okholm and Timothy R. Phillips. Grand Rapids, Mich.: Zondervan, 1995.

Frey, Jörg. *Die johanneische Eschatologie.* 3 vols. Wissenschaftliche Untersuchungen zum Neuen Testament 96, 110, 177. Tübingen: Mohr Siebeck, 1997-2000.

Fudge, Edward. *The Fire That Consumes: The Biblical Case for Conditional Immortality.* 2d ed. Carlisle, U.K.: Paternoster, 1994.

The Fundamentalist Phenomenon: The Resurgence of Conservative Christianity. Edited by Jerry Falwell with Ed Dobson and Ed Hinson. Garden City, N.Y.: Doubleday, 1981.

The Fundamentals: A Testimony to the Truth. 4 vols. Los Angeles: Bible Institute of Los Angeles, 1917.

Funk, R. W. "Papyrus Bodmer II (P[66]) and John 8, 25." *Harvard Theological Review* 51 (1958): 95-100.

Gese, Hartmut. *Essays on Biblical Theology.* Translated by Keith Crim. Minneapolis: Augsburg, 1981.

Gieschen, Charles A. *Angelomorphic Christology: Antecedents and Early Evidence.* Arbeiten zur Geschichte des antiken Judentums und des Urchristentums 42. Leiden: Brill, 1988.

Godet, F. *Commentary on the Gospel of John: With an Historical and Critical Introduction.* Translated by Timothy Dwight. 2 vols. New York: Funk & Wagnalls, 1886.

Golding, John. *Paths to the Absolute: Mondrian, Malevich, Kandinsky, Pollock, Newman, Rothko, and Still.* The A. W. Mellon Lectures in the Fine Arts, 1997; Bollington Series 35/48. Princeton, N.J.: Princeton University Press, 2000.

Goode, Erich. "Further Reflections on the Church-Sect Dimension." *Journal for the Scientific Study of Religion* 6 (1967): 270-275.

————. "Some Critical Observations on the Church-Sect Dimension." *Journal for the Scientific Study of Religion* 6 (1967): 69-77.

Greek-English Lexicon of the New Testament: Based on Semantic Domains. Edited by J. P. Louw and E. A. Nida. 2 vols. 2d ed. New York: United Bible Societies, 1989.

Grenz, Stanley J. *Renewing the Center: Evangelical Theology in a Post-Theological Era.* A Bridgepoint Book. Grand Rapids, Mich.: Baker, 2000.

Gundry, Robert H. "Angelomorphic Christology in the Book of Revelation." Pages 662-678 in *SBL Seminar Papers, 1994.* Society of Biblical Literature Seminar Papers 33. Atlanta: Scholars Press, 1994.

————. "Reconstructing Jesus." *Christianity Today* 42/5 (April 27, 1998): 76-79.

Gustafson, James M. "The Sectarian Temptation: Reflections on Theology, the Church and the University." *Proceedings of the Catholic Theological Society* 40 (1985): 83-94.

Gustafson, Paul. "UO-US-PS-PO: A Restatement of Troeltsch's Church-Sect Typology." *Journal for the Scientific Study of Religion* 6 (1967): 64-68.

Halliday, Michael A. K. "Anti-languages." *American Anthropologist* 78 (1976): 570-584.

————. *Language as Social Semiotic: The Social Interpretation of Language and Meaning.* London: Edward Arnold, 1978.

Hamid-Khani, Saeed. *Revelation and Concealment of Christ: A Theological Inquiry into the Elusive Language of the Fourth Gospel.* Wissenschaftliche Untersuchungen zum Neuen Testament 2/120. Tübingen: Mohr Siebeck, 2000.

Hamilton, Michael S. "More Money, More Ministry: The Financing of American Evangelicalism since 1945." Pages 104-138 in *More Money, More Ministry: Money and Evangelicalism in Recent North American History.* Edited by Larry Eskridge and Mark A. Noll. Grand Rapids, Mich.: Eerdmans, 2000.

―――. "We're in the Money! How Did Evangelicals Get So Wealthy, and What Has It Done to Us?" *Christianity Today* 44/7 (June 12, 2000): 36-43.

Hammond, Phillip E., and James Davison Hunter. "On Maintaining Plausibility: The Worldview of Evangelical College Students." *Journal for the Scientific Study of Religion* 23 (1984): 221-238.

Hanson, Anthony Tyrrell. "John's Citation of Psalm LXXXII." *New Testament Studies* 11 (1964-1965): 158-162.

―――. "John's Citation of Psalm LXXXII Reconsidered." *New Testament Studies* 13 (1966-1967): 363-367.

―――. *The Prophetic Gospel: A Study of John and the Old Testament.* Edinburgh: T&T Clark, 1991.

Harnack, Adolf. "Ueber das Verhältnis des Prologs des vierten Evangeliums zum ganzen Werk." *Zeitschrift für Theologie und Kirche* 2 (1892): 189-231.

Harris, Elizabeth. *Prologue and Gospel: The Theology of the Fourth Evangelist.* Journal for the Study of the New Testament: Supplement Series 107. Sheffield: Sheffield Academic Press, 1994.

Harvey, A. E. *Jesus on Trial: A Study in the Fourth Gospel.* Atlanta: John Knox, 1977.

Hatch, Nathan O., and Michael S. Hamilton. "Can Evangelicalism Survive Its Success?" *Christianity Today* 36/11 (Oct. 5, 1992): 21-31.

Hauerwas, Stanley M. *Christian Existence Today: Essays on Church, World, and Living In Between.* Durham, N.C.: Labyrinth, 1988.

Hauerwas, Stanley M., and William H. Willimon. *Resident Aliens: Life in the Christian Colony.* Nashville: Abingdon, 1989.

Hays, Richard B. *The Moral Vision of the New Testament: A Contemporary Introduction to New Testament Ethics.* New York: HarperCollins, 1996.

Head, Peter M. "The Duration of Divine Judgment in the New Testament." Pages 221-227 in *Eschatology in Bible and Theology: Evangelical Essays at the Dawn of a New Millennium.* Edited by Kent E. Brower and Mark W. Elliott. Downers Grove, Ill.: InterVarsity, 1997.

Hengel, Martin. "Die Schriftauslegung des 4. Evangeliums auf Hintergrund der urchristlichen Exegese." *Jahrbuch für Biblische Theologie* 4 (1989): 249-288.

Hesselgrave, David. "Evangelical Mission in 2001 and Beyond — Who Will Set the Agenda?" *Trinity World Forum* 26/2 (Spring, 2001): 1-3.

Higgins, A. J. B. "The Words of Jesus according to St. John." *Bulletin of the John Rylands University Library of Manchester* 49 (1966-1967): 363-386.

Hinrichs, Boy. *"Ich Bin": Die Konsistenz des Johannes-Evangeliums in der Konzentration auf des Wort Jesus.* Stuttgarter Bibelstudien 133. Stuttgart: Katholisches Bibelwerk, 1988.

Hoegen-Rohls, Christina. *Der nachösterliche Johannes: Die Abschiedsreden als hermeneutischer Schlüssel zum vierten Evangelium.* Wissenschaftliche Untersuchungen zum Neuen Testament 2/84. Tübingen: Mohr (Siebeck), 1996.

Hofius, Otfried. "'Er gibt den Geist ohne Mass' Joh 3,34b." *Zeitschrift für die neutestamentliche Wissenschaft und die Kunde der älteren Kirche* 90 (1999): 131-134.

Holmberg, Bengt. *Sociology and the New Testament: An Appraisal.* Minneapolis: Fortress, 1990.

Holmes, Arthur F. *The Idea of a Christian College.* 2d ed. Grand Rapids, Mich.: Eerdmans, 1987.

Holtzmann, H. J. *Evangelium, Briefe und Offenbarung des Johannes.* 2d ed. Handkommentar zum Neuen Testament 4. Freiburg im Breisgau: Mohr-Siebeck, 1893.

Horbury, William. *Jewish Messianism and the Cult of Christ.* London: SCM, 1998.

———. *Jews and Christians in Contact and Controversy.* Edinburgh: T&T Clark, 1998.

Huebner, Harry J. "Moral Agency as Embodiment: How the Church Acts." Pages 189-212 in *The Wisdom of the Cross: Essays in Honor of John Howard Yoder.* Edited by Stanley Hauerwas, Chris K. Huebner, Harry J. Huebner, and Mark Thiessen Nation. Grand Rapids, Mich.: Eerdmans, 1999.

Huffman, Joseph P. "Faith, Reason, and the Text: The Return of the Middle Ages to Postmodern Scholarship." *Christian Scholar's Review* 29 (1999): 281-301.

Hultgren, Arland J. *The Rise of Normative Christianity.* Minneapolis: Augsburg Fortress, 1994.

Hunter, James Davison. *American Evangelicalism: Conservative Religion and the Quandary of Modernity.* New Brunswick: Rutgers University Press, 1983.

———. "Breaking Traditions: Fin de Siècle 1896 and 1996." *Partisan Review* 64 (1997): 187-196, 212.

———. "Conservative Protestantism." Pages 150-166 in *The Sacred in a Secular Age: Toward Revision in the Scientific Study of Religion.* Edited by Phillip E. Hammond. Berkeley: University of California Press, 1985.

————. *Evangelicalism: The Coming Generation.* Chicago: University of Chicago Press, 1987.

————. "The New Class and the Young Evangelicals." *Review of Religious Research* 22 (1980-1981): 155-169.

————. "The Perils of Idealism: A Reply." *Review of Religious Research* 24 (1982-1983): 267-276.

————. "Subjectivization and the New Evangelical Theodicy." *Journal for the Scientific Study of Religion* 21 (1982): 39-47.

Huyssen, Andreas. *After the Great Divide: Modernity, Mass Culture, Postmodernism.* Theories of Representation and Difference. Bloomington, Ind.: Indiana University Press, 1986.

————. "Mapping the Postmodern." Pages 40-72 in *The Post-Modern Reader.* Edited by Charles Jencks. New York: St. Martin's Press, 1992.

Jackson, Howard M. "Ancient Self-Referential Conventions and Their Implications for the Authorship and Integrity of the Gospel of John." *Journal of Theological Studies* new series 50 (1999): 1-34.

Jencks, Charles. "The Post-Modern Agenda." Pages 10-39 in *The Post-Modern Reader.* Edited by Charles Jencks. New York: St. Martin's Press, 1992.

Jobes, Karen H. "Sophia Christology: The Way of Wisdom?" Pages 226-250 in *The Way of Wisdom: Essays in Honor of Bruce K. Waltke.* Edited by J. I. Packer and Sven K. Soderlund. Grand Rapids, Mich.: Zondervan, 2000.

Johnson, Benton. "Church and Sect Revisited." *Journal for the Scientific Study of Religion* 10 (1971): 124-137.

————. "A Critical Appraisal of Church-Sect Typology." *American Sociological Review* 22 (1957): 88-92.

————. "On Church and Sect." *American Sociological Review* 28 (1963): 539-549.

Johnstone, Ronald L. *Religion in Society: A Sociology of Religion.* 5th ed. Upper Saddle River, N.J.: Prentice-Hall, 1997.

Jonge, Marinus de. *Jesus Stranger from Heaven and Son of God: Jesus Christ and the Christians in Johannine Perspective.* Society of Biblical Literature Sources for Biblical Study 11. Missoula, Mont.: Scholars Press, 1977.

Jungkuntz, Richard. "An Approach to the Exegesis of John 10:34-36." *Concordia Theological Monthly* 35 (1964): 556-565.

Kammler, Hans-Christian. *Christologie und Eschatologie: Joh 5, 17-30 als Schlüsseltext johanneischer Theologie.* Wissenschaftliche Untersuchungen zum Neuen Testament 126. Tübingen: Mohr Siebeck, 2000.

————. "Jesus Christus und der Geistparaklet: Eine Studie zur johanneische Verhältnisbestimmung von Pneumatologie und Christologie." Pages 170-181 in Otfried Hofius and Hans-Christian Kammler, *Johannesstudien: Un-*

tersuchungen zur Theologie des vierten Evangeliums. Wissenschaftliche Untersuchungen zum Neuen Testament 88. Tübingen: Mohr-Siebeck, 1996.

Kanagaraj, Jey J. "Jesus the King, Merkabah Mysticism, and the Gospel of John." *Tyndale Bulletin* 47 (1996): 349-366.

Kandinsky, Wassily. *Concerning the Spiritual in Art.* Translated by M. T. H. Sadler. New York: Dover, 1977.

Käsemann, Ernst. *The Testament of Jesus: A Study of the Gospel of John in the Light of Chapter 17.* Translated by Gerhard Krodel. Philadelphia: Fortress, 1968.

Kee, Howard Clark. *Knowing the Truth: A Sociological Approach to the New Testament.* Minneapolis: Fortress, 1989.

Kelber, Werner H. "The Authority of the Word in St. John's Gospel: Charismatic Speech, Narrative Text, Logocentric Metaphysics." *Oral Tradition* 2 (1987): 108-131.

————. "The Birth of a Beginning: John 1.1-18." Pages 209-230 in *The Gospel of John as Literature: An Anthology of Twentieth-Century Perspectives.* New Testament Tools and Studies 17. Leiden: Brill, 1993.

————. "Die Fleischwerdung des Wortes in der Körperlichkeit des Textes." Pages 31-42 in *Materialität der Kommunikation.* Edited by Hans Ulrich Gumbrecht and K. Ludwig Pfeiffer. Suhrkamp Taschenbuch Wissenschaft 70. Frankfurt am Main: Suhrkamp, 1988.

————. "In the Beginning Were the Words: The Apotheosis and Narrative Displacement of the Logos." *Journal of the American Academy of Religion* 58 (1990): 69-98.

Kelley, Dean M. *Why Conservative Churches Are Growing: A Study in Sociology of Religion.* New York: Harper & Row, 1972.

Kermode, Frank. "John." Pages 440-466 in *The Literary Guide to the Bible.* Edited by Robert Alter and Frank Kermode. Cambridge, Mass.: Harvard University Press, 1987.

Kim, Dongsoo. "The Church in the Gospel of John." *Tyndale Bulletin* 50 (1999): 314-317.

Kittel, G., and G. Friedrich, eds. *Theological Dictionary of the New Testament.* Translated by G. W. Bromiley. 10 vols. Grand Rapids, Mich.: Eerdmans, 1964-1976.

Klassen, William. "Παρρησία in the Johannine Corpus." Pages 227-254 in *Friendship, Flattery, and Frankness of Speech: Studies in Friendship in the New Testament World.* Edited by John T. Fitzgerald. Supplements to Novum Testamentum 82. Leiden: Brill, 1996.

Klauck, Hans-Josef. "Brudermord und Bruderliebe: Ethische Paradigmen in

1 Joh 3,11-17." Pages 151-169 in *Neues Testament und Ethik*. Edited by Helmut Merklein. Freiburg: Herder, 1989.

Klotz, Heinrich. "Postmodern Architecture." Pages 234-248 in *The Post-Modern Reader*. Edited by Charles Jencks. New York: St. Martin's Press, 1992.

Knudsen, Dean D., John R. Earle, and Donald W. Shriver Jr. "The Conception of Sectarian Religion: An Effort at Clarification." *Review of Religious Research* 20 (1978-79): 44-60.

Köstenberger, Andreas J. "Jesus as Rabbi in the Fourth Gospel." *Bulletin for Biblical Research* 8 (1998): 97-128.

Kowalski, Beate. *Die Hirtenrede (Joh 10, 1-18) im Kontext des Johannesevangelium.* Stuttgart: Katholisches Bibelwerk, 1996.

Kysar, Robert. "Coming Hermeneutical Earthquake in Johannine Interpretation." Pages 185-189 in *"What Is John?" Readers and Readings of the Fourth Gospel.* Edited by Fernando F. Segovia. Society of Biblical Literature Symposium Series 3. Atlanta: Scholars Press, 1996.

————. *John.* Augsburg Commentaries on the New Testament. Minneapolis: Augsburg, 1986.

————. *Stumbling in the Light: New Testament Images for a Changing Church.* St. Louis: Chalice, 1999.

Lagrange, M.-J. *Évangile selon Saint Jean.* 5th ed. Études bibliques. Paris: Gabalda, 1936.

Lakeland, Paul. *Postmodernity: Christian Identity in a Fragmented Age.* Guides to Theological Inquiry. Minneapolis: Fortress, 1997.

Lawson, Matthew P. "Sects and Churches, Conservatives and Liberals: Shades of Max Weber in the Sociology of Religion in America, 1904-1993." *Research in the Social Scientific Study of Religion* 6 (1994): 1-33.

Lenski, R. C. H. *The Interpretation of St. John's Gospel.* Columbus, Ohio: Wartburg, 1942.

Leroy, Herbert. *Rätsel und Missverständnis: Ein Beitrag zur Formgeschichte des Johannesevangeliums.* Bonner biblische Beiträge 30. Bonn: Peter Hanstein, 1968.

Lewis, C. S. *The Last Battle.* New York: Macmillan, 1956.

Liddell, Henry George, Robert Scott, and Henry Stuart Jones. *A Greek-English Lexicon.* 9th ed. with a revised supplement. Oxford: Clarendon, 1996.

Lightfoot, R. H. *Saint John's Gospel: A Commentary.* Edited by C. F. Evans. Oxford: Clarendon, 1956.

Lindars, Barnabas. *Behind the Fourth Gospel.* Studies in Creative Criticism 3. London: SPCK, 1971.

————. "Discourse and Tradition: The Use of the Sayings of Jesus in the Discourses of the Fourth Gospel." *Journal for the Study of the New Testament* 13 (1981): 83-101.

———. *The Gospel of John.* New Century Bible. London: Oliphants, 1972.

Lindbeck, George A. *The Nature of Doctrine: Religion and Theology in a Postliberal Age.* Philadelphia: Westminster, 1984.

———. "The Sectarian Future of the Church." Pages 226-243 in *The God Experience: Essays in Hope.* Edited by Joseph P. Whelan. The Cardinal Bea Lectures 2. New York: Newman, 1971.

Link, Andrea. *"Was redest du mit ihr?": Eine Studie zur Exegese-, Redaktions-, und Theologiegeschichte von Joh 4, 1-42.* Biblische Untersuchungen 24. Regensburg: Pustet, 1992.

Littell, Franklin Hamlin. *The Anabaptist View of the Church.* Boston: Starr King, 1958.

———. "The Social Background of the Anabaptist View of the Church." Pages 230-237 in *Sociology and Religion: A Book of Readings.* Edited by Norman Birnbaum and Gertrud Lenzer. Englewood Cliffs, N.J.: Prentice-Hall, 1969.

Lucas, Sean Michael. "Fundamentalisms Revived and Still Standing: A Review Essay." *Westminster Theological Journal* 60 (1998): 327-337.

Malina, Bruce J. "The Gospel of John in Sociolinguistic Perspective." *Protocol of the Colloquy of the Center for Hermeneutical Studies in Hellenistic and Modern Culture.* Colloquy 48. Berkeley: Center for Hermeneutical Studies, 1985.

Malina, Bruce J., and Richard L. Rohrbaugh. *Social-Science Commentary on the Gospel of John.* Minneapolis: Fortress, 1998.

Marsden, George. *Understanding Fundamentalism and Evangelicalism.* Grand Rapids, Mich.: Eerdmans, 1991.

Marty, Martin E. "Tensions within Contemporary Evangelicalism: A Critical Appraisal." Pages 170-188 in *The Evangelicals: What They Believe, Who They Are, Where They Are Changing.* Edited by David F. Wells and John D. Woodbridge. Nashville: Abingdon, 1975.

Marxsen, Willi. *New Testament Foundations for Christian Ethics.* Translated by O. C. Dean Jr. Minneapolis: Fortress, 1993.

Mayers, Marvin K., Lawrence O. Richards, and Robert Webber. *Reshaping Evangelical Higher Education.* Grand Rapids, Mich.: Zondervan, 1972.

McKnight, Scot. *A New Vision for Israel: The Teachings of Jesus in National Context.* Grand Rapids, Mich.: Eerdmans, 1999.

Meeks, Wayne A. "The Ethics of the Fourth Evangelist." Pages 317-326 in *Exploring the Gospel of John.* Edited by R. Alan Culpepper and C. Clifton Black. Louisville, Ky.: Westminster John Knox, 1996.

———. "The Man from Heaven in Johannine Sectarianism." *Journal of Biblical Literature* 91 (1972): 44-72.

Meier, John P. *A Marginal Jew: Rethinking the Historical Jesus.* 2 vols. published of 3 vols. projected. Anchor Bible Reference Library. New York: Doubleday, 1991-.

Menken, M. J. J. "The Christology of the Fourth Gospel: A Survey of Recent Research." Pages 292-320 in *From Jesus to John: Essays on Jesus and New Testament Christology in Honour of Marinus de Jonge.* Edited by Martinus De Boer. Journal for the Study of the New Testament: Supplement Series 84. Sheffield: Sheffield Academic Press, 1993.

———. "The Use of the Septuagint in Three Quotations in John: Jn 10,34; 12,38; 19,24." Pages 367-393 in *The Scriptures in the Gospels.* Edited by C. M. Tuckett. Bibliotheca ephemeridum theologicarum lovaniensium 131. Leuven: Leuven University Press, 1997.

Metzger, Bruce M. *A Textual Commentary on the Greek New Testament.* 3d ed. London: United Bible Societies, 1971.

Milbank, John. *Theology and Social Theory: Beyond Secular Reason.* Oxford: Blackwell, 1990.

Miller, Donald E. "Sectarianism and Secularization: The Work of Bryan Wilson." *Religious Studies Review* 5 (1979): 161-174.

Miller, Ed. L. "The Christology of John 8:25." *Theologische Zeitschrift* 36 (1980): 257-265.

———. "The Johannine Origins of the Johannine Logos." *Journal of Biblical Literature* 112 (1993): 445-457.

Moberg, David O. "Fundamentalists and Evangelicals in Society." Pages 143-169 in *The Evangelicals: What They Believe, Who They Are, Where They Are Changing.* Edited by David F. Wells and John D. Woodbridge. Nashville: Abingdon, 1975.

———. *The Great Reversal: Evangelicalism versus Social Concern.* Evangelical Perspectives. Philadelphia: Lippincott, 1972.

Moloney, Francis J. *Belief in the Word: Reading the Fourth Gospel: John 1–4.* Minneapolis: Fortress, 1993.

———. *The Gospel of John.* Sacra pagina 4. Collegeville, Minn.: Liturgical Press, 1998.

Montefiore, H. "Thou Shalt Love Thy Neighbor as Thyself." *Novum Testamentum* 5 (1962): 157-170.

Moule, C. F. D. *The Origin of Christology.* Cambridge: Cambridge University Press, 1977.

Mouw, Richard J. *The Smell of Sawdust: What Evangelicals Can Learn from Their Fundamentalist Heritage.* Grand Rapids, Mich.: Zondervan, 2000.

Müller, Theophil. *Das Heilsgeschehen im Johannesevangelium: Eine exegetische Studie, zugleich der Versuch einer Antwort an Rudolf Bultmann.* Frankfurt am Main: Gotthelf-Verlag, 1961.

Neyrey, Jerome H. "'I Said: You Are Gods': Psalm 82:6 and John 10." *Journal of Biblical Literature* 108 (1989): 647-663.

———. *An Ideology of Revolt: John's Christology in Social-Science Perspective.* Philadelphia: Fortress, 1988.

———. "The Sociology of Secrecy and the Fourth Gospel." Pages 79-109 in *"What Is John?"* Vol. 2: *Literary and Social Readings of the Fourth Gospel.* Edited by Fernando F. Segovia. Society of Biblical Literature Symposium Series 7. Atlanta: Scholars Press, 1998.

Niebuhr, H. Richard. *Christ and Culture.* Harper Torchbooks. New York: Harper & Brothers, 1951.

———. *The Social Sources of Denominationalism.* New York: Henry Holt, 1929.

Nissan, Johannes. "Community and Ethics in the Gospel of John." Pages 194-212 in *New Readings in John: Literary and Theological Perspectives: Essays from the Scandinavian Conference on the Fourth Gospel, Aarhus 1997.* Edited by Johannes Nissan and Sigfred Pedersen. Journal for the Study of the New Testament: Supplement Series 182. Sheffield: Sheffield Academic Press, 1999.

Noll, Mark A. *The Scandal of the Evangelical Mind.* Grand Rapids, Mich.: Eerdmans, 1994.

Obermann, Andreas. *Die christologische Erfüllung der Schrift im Johannesevangelium: Eine Untersuchung zur johanneischen Hermeneutik anhand der Schriftzitate.* Wissenschaftliche Untersuchungen zum Neuen Testament 2/83. Tübingen: Mohr-Siebeck, 1996.

O'Day, Gail R. *Revelation in the Fourth Gospel: Narrative Mode and Theological Claim.* Philadelphia: Fortress, 1986.

Oden, Thomas C. *After Modernity . . . What?* Grand Rapids, Mich.: Zondervan, 1990.

Olsson, Birger. *Structure and Meaning in the Fourth Gospel: A Text-Linguistic Analysis of John 2:1-11 and 4:1-42.* Coniectanea biblica: New Testament Series 6. Lund: Gleerup, 1974.

Østenstad, Gunnar H. *Patterns of Redemption in the Fourth Gospel: An Experiment in Structural Analysis.* Studies in the Bible and Early Christianity 38. Lewiston, N.Y.: Mellen, 1998.

Painter, John. "Inclined to God: The Quest for Eternal Life — Bultmannian

Hermeneutics and the Theology of the Fourth Gospel." Pages 346-368 in *Exploring the Gospel of John*. Edited by R. Alan Culpepper and C. Clifton Black. Louisville, Ky.: Westminster John Knox, 1996.

―――. "Johannine Symbols: A Case Study in Epistemology." *Journal of Theology for Southern Africa* 27 (1979): 26-41.

―――. *The Quest for the Messiah: The History, Literature, and Theology of the Johannine Community*. 2d ed. Nashville: Abingdon, 1993.

―――. *Reading John's Gospel Today*. Atlanta: John Knox, 1975.

Passow, Franz. *Handwörterbuch der griechischen Sprache*. 4 vols. Leipzig: Fr. Chr. Wilh. Vogel, 1852.

Pertini, M. A. "La genialidad grammatical de Jn 8, 25." *Estudios biblicos* 56 (1998): 371-408.

Petersen, Norman R. *The Gospel of John and the Sociology of Light: Language and Characterization in the Fourth Gospel*. Valley Forge, Pa.: Trinity Press International, 1993.

Peterson, Robert A. "Undying Worm, Unquenchable Fire." *Christianity Today* 44/12 (Oct. 23, 2000): 30-37.

Pilgaard, Aage. "The Qumran Scrolls and John's Gospel." Pages 126-142 in *New Readings in John: Literary and Theological Perspectives: Essays from the Scandinavian Conference on the Fourth Gospel, Aarhus 1997*. Edited by Johannes Nissen and Sigfred Pedersen. Journal for the Study of the New Testament: Supplement Series 182. Sheffield: Sheffield Academic Press, 1999.

Pinnock, Clark H. *Flame of Love: A Theology of the Holy Spirit*. Downers Grove, Ill.: InterVarsity Press, 1996.

―――. *A Wideness in God's Mercy: The Finality of Jesus Christ in a World of Religions*. Grand Rapids, Mich.: Zondervan, 1992.

Piper, John. *Let the Nations Be Glad! The Supremacy of God in Missions*. Grand Rapids, Mich.: Baker, 1993.

Platonis Dialogi secundum Thrasylli Tetralogias. Edited by C. F. Hermann. 6 vols. Leipzig: Teubner, 1892.

Pope, Liston. *Millhands and Preachers: A Study of Gastonia*. New Haven: Yale University Press, 1942.

Porsch, Felix. *Anwalt der Glaubenden: Das Wirken des Geistes nach dem Zeugnis des Johannesevangeliums*. Geist und Leben. Stuttgart: Katholisches Bibelwerk, 1978.

―――. *Pneuma und Wort*. Frankfurter Theologische Studien 16. Frankfurt: Knecht, 1974.

Portoghesi, Paolo. "What Is the Postmodern?" Pages 208-214 in *The Post-Modern Reader*. Edited by Charles Jencks. New York: St. Martin's Press, 1992.

Potterie, Ignace de la. "'C'est lui qui a ouvert la voie': La finale du prologue johannique." *Biblica* 69 (1988): 340-370.

———. "La notion de 'commencement' dans les écrits johanniques." Pages 386-389 in *Die Kirche des Anfangs*. Edited by Rudolf Schnackenburg, Josef Ernst, and Joachim Wanke. Erfurter theologische Studien 38. Leipzig: St. Benno-Verlag, 1977.

———. *La vérité dans Saint Jean*. 2 vols. Analecta biblica 73-74. Rome: Biblical Institute Press, 1977.

Pryor, J. W. "Covenant and Community in John's Gospel." *Reformed Theological Review* 47 (1988): 44-51.

Quebedeaux, Richard. *The Worldly Evangelicals*. New York: Harper & Row, 1978.

Redekop, Calvin. "The Sect Cycle in Perspective." *Mennonite Quarterly Review* 36 (1962): 155-161.

Reese, Boyd. "The New Class and the Young Evangelicals — Second Thoughts." *Review of Religious Research* 24 (1982-1983): 261-267.

Reim, Günter. "Joh. 8.44 — Gotteskinder/Teufelskinder. Wie antijudaistisch ist 'Die wohl antijudaistischste Äusserung des NT'?" *New Testament Studies* 30 (1984): 619-624.

Reinhartz, Adele. "Jesus as Prophet: Predictive Prolepses in the Fourth Gospel." *Journal for the Study of the New Testament* 36 (1989): 3-16.

Rensberger, David. *Johannine Faith and Liberating Community*. Philadelphia: Westminster, 1988.

———. "Sectarianism and Theological Interpretation in John." Pages 139-156 in *"What Is John?"* Vol. 2: *Literary and Social Readings of the Fourth Gospel*. Edited by Fernando F. Segovia. Society of Biblical Literature Symposium Series 7. Atlanta: Scholars Press, 1998.

Ridderbos, Herman N. *The Gospel according to John: A Theological Commentary*. Translated by John Vriend. Grand Rapids, Mich.: Eerdmans, 1997.

Rieff, Philip. *The Triumph of the Therapeutic: Uses of Faith After Freud*. Harper Torchbooks. New York: Harper & Row, 1966.

Robert, René. "La double intention du mot final du prologue johannique." *Revue Thomiste* 87 (1987): 435-441.

———. "Le mot final du prologue johannique: À propos d'un article récent." *Revue Thomiste* 89 (1989): 279-288.

———. "Un précédent platonicien à l'équivoque de Jean 1, 18." *Revue Thomiste* 90 (1990): 634-639.

Roberts, Keith A. *Religion in Sociological Perspective*. The Dorsey Series in Sociology. Homewood, Ill.: Dorsey, 1984.

Robinson, John A. T. *The Priority of John.* Edited by J. F. Coakley. London: SCM, 1985.

―――. *Twelve More New Testament Studies.* London: SCM, 1984.

Robinson, Thomas A. *The Bauer Thesis Examined: The Geography of Heresy in the Early Christian Church.* Lewiston, N.Y.: Edwin Mellen, 1988.

Rohrbaugh, Richard L. "The Gospel of John in the Twenty-First Century." Pages 257-363 in *"What Is John?"* Vol. 2: *Literary and Social Readings of the Fourth Gospel.* Edited by Fernando F. Segovia. Society of Biblical Literature Symposium Series 7. Atlanta: Scholars Press, 1998.

Roof, Wade Clark, and William McKinney. *American Mainline Religion: Its Changing Shape and Future.* New Brunswick, N.J.: Rutgers University Press, 1987.

Rookmaaker, H. R. *Modern Art and the Death of a Culture.* 2d ed. Downers Grove, Ill.: InterVarsity Press, 1973.

Roozen, David A., and C. Kirk Hadaway. *Church and Denominational Growth.* Nashville: Abingdon, 1993.

Rowland, Christopher. *Christian Origins: From Messianic Movement to Christian Religion.* Minneapolis: Augsburg, 1985.

―――. "John 1. 51, Jewish Apocalyptic and Targumic Tradition." *New Testament Studies* 30 (1984): 498-507.

Sanders, E. P. *The Historical Figure of Jesus.* London: Penguin, 1993.

―――. *Jesus and Judaism.* Philadelphia: Fortress, 1985.

Sanders, Jack T. *Ethics in the New Testament.* Philadelphia: Fortress, 1975.

―――. *Schismatics, Sectarians, Dissidents, Deviants: The First One Hundred Years of Jewish-Christian Relations.* Valley Forge, Pa.: Trinity Press International, 1993.

Sanders, John. *No Other Name: An Investigation into the Destiny of the Unevangelized.* Grand Rapids, Mich.: Eerdmans, 1992.

Sargeant, Kimon Howland. *Seeker Churches: Promoting Traditional Religion in a Nontraditional Way.* New Brunswick, N.J.: Rutgers University Press, 2000.

Schäufele, Wolfgang. *Das missionarische Bewusstsein und Wirken der Täufer.* Beiträge zur Geschichte und Lehre der Reformierten Kirche 21. Neukirchen: Verlag des Erziehungsvereins, 1966.

Schlier, Heinrich. *Das Ende der Zeit: Exegetische Aufsätze und Vorträge III.* Freiburg: Herder, 1971.

Schnackenburg, Rudolf. *The Gospel according to St John, Volume One: Introduction and Commentary on Chapters 1–4.* Translated by Kevin Smyth. Herder's Theological Commentary on the New Testament. New York: Herder and Herder, 1968.

―――. *The Gospel according to St John, Volume Two: Commentary on Chapters*

5–12. Translated by Cecily Hastings, Francis McDonagh, David Smith, and Richard Foley. A Crossroad Book. New York: Seabury, 1980.

————. *The Gospel according to St John, Volume Three: Commentary on Chapters 13–21.* Translated by David Smith and G. A. Kon. Herder's Theological Commentary on the New Testament. New York: Crossroad, 1982.

————. *The Johannine Epistles: Introduction and Commentary.* Translated by Reginald and Ilse Fuller. New York: Crossroad, 1992.

————. *The Moral Teaching of the New Testament.* Translated by J. Holland-Smith and W. J. O'Hara. New York: Herder, 1965.

Schnelle, Udo. *Antidocetic Christology in the Gospel of John: An Investigation of the Place of the Fourth Gospel in the Johannine School.* Translated by Linda M. Maloney. Minneapolis: Fortress, 1992.

Scholtissek, K. "Abschied und Neue Gegenwart: Exegetische und theologische Reflexionen zur johanneischen Abschiedsrede 13,31–17,26." *Ephemerides theologicae lovanienses* 75 (1999): 332-358.

Schuchard, Bruce G. *Scripture within Scripture: The Interrelationship of Form and Function in the Explicit Old Testament Citations in the Gospel of John.* Society of Biblical Literature Dissertation Series 133. Atlanta: Scholars Press, 1992.

Schulz, Siegfried. *Untersuchungen zur Menschensohn-Christologie im Johannesevangelium: Zugleich ein Beitrag zur Methodengeschichte der Auslegung des 4. Evangeliums.* Göttingen: Vandenhoeck & Ruprecht, 1957.

Scott, Martin. *Sophia and the Johannine Jesus.* Journal for the Study of the New Testament: Supplement Series 71. Sheffield: Sheffield Academic Press, 1992.

Scroggs, Robin. "The Earliest Christian Communities as Sectarian Movements." Pages 69-91 in *Social-Scientific Approaches to New Testament Interpretation.* Edited by David G. Horrell. Edinburgh: T&T Clark, 1999.

Segovia, Fernando F. "The Gospel at the Close of the Century: Engagement from the Diaspora." Pages 211-216 in *"What Is John?" Readers and Readings of the Fourth Gospel.* Edited by Fernando F. Segovia. Society of Biblical Literature Symposium Series 3. Atlanta: Scholars Press, 1996.

Smalley, Stephen S. "Johannes 1,51 und die Einleitung zum vierten Evangelium." Pages 300-313 in *Jesus und der Menschensohn.* Edited by Rudolf Pesch and Rudolf Schnackenburg with Odilo Kaiser. Freiburg: Herder, 1975.

Smith, Christian, with Michael Emerson, Sally Gallagher, Paul Kennedy, and David Sikkink. *American Evangelicalism: Embattled and Thriving.* Chicago: University of Chicago Press, 1998.

Smith, Christian. *Christian America? What Evangelicals Really Want.* Berkeley: University of California Press, 2000.

133

Smothers, E. R. "Two Readings in Papyrus Bodmer II." *Harvard Theological Review* 51 (1958): 111-122.

Söding, Thomas. "'Was kann aus Nazareth schon Gutes kommen?' (Joh 1.46): Die Bedeutung des Judesein Jesu im Johannesevangelium." *New Testament Studies* 46 (2000): 21-41.

Spicq, Ceslas. *Theological Lexicon of the New Testament*. Translated and edited by James D. Ernest. 3 vols. Peabody, Mass.: Hendrickson, 1994.

Stanley, John E. "The Apocalypse and Contemporary Sect Analysis." Pages 412-421 in *SBL Seminar Papers, 1986*. Society of Biblical Literature Seminar Papers 25. Atlanta: Scholars Press, 1986.

Stark, Rodney. "Church and Sect." Pages 139-149 in *The Sacred in a Secular Age: Toward Revision in the Scientific Study of Religion*. Edited by Phillip E. Hammond. Berkeley: University of California Press, 1985.

Stark, Rodney, and William Sims Bainbridge. *The Future of Religion: Secularization, Revival and Cult Formation*. Berkeley: University of California Press, 1985.

Stark, Werner. *The Sociology of Religion: A Study of Christendom*. 5 vols. New York: Fordham University Press, 1966-1972.

Stone, Jon R. *On the Boundaries of American Evangelicalism: The Postwar Evangelical Coalition*. New York: St. Martin's Press, 1997.

Stowers, Stanley Kent. "The Social Sciences and the Study of Early Christianity." Pages 149-181 in *Approaches to Ancient Judaism*. Vol. 5: *Studies in Judaism and Its Greco-Roman Context*. Edited by William Scott Green. Brown Judaic Studies 32. Atlanta: Scholars Press, 1985.

Strange, Daniel. "Clark H. Pinnock: The Evolution of an Evangelical Maverick." *Evangelical Quarterly* 7 (1999): 311-326.

Strecker, Georg. *Theology of the New Testament*. German edition edited and completed by Friedrich Wilhelm Horn. Translated by M. Eugene Boring. New York: Walter de Gruyter, 2000.

Stuckenbruck, Loren T. *Angel Veneration and Christology: A Study in Early Judaism and in the Christology of the Apocalypse of John*. Wissenschaftliche Untersuchungen zum Neuen Testament 2/70. Tübingen: Mohr (Siebeck), 1995.

Suh, Joong Suk. *The Glory in the Gospel: Restoration of Forfeited Prestige*. Oxford, Ohio: M. P. Publications, 1995.

Tenney, Merrill C. "The Gospel of John." Pages 1-203 in vol. 9 of *Expositor's Bible Commentary*. Regency Reference Library. Grand Rapids, Mich.: Zondervan, 1981.

Theobald, Michael. *Die Fleischwerdung des Logos: Studien zum Verhältnis des Jo-*

hannesprologs zum Corpus des Evangeliums und zu 1 Joh. Neutestamentliche Abhandlungen new series 20. Münster: Aschendorff, 1988.

Theological Dictionary of the New Testament. Edited by G. Kittel and G. Friedrich. Translated by G. W. Bromiley. 10 vols. Grand Rapids, Mich.: Eerdmans, 1964-1976.

Thompson, Marianne Meye. *The Incarnate Word: Perspectives on Jesus in the Fourth Gospel.* Peabody, Mass.: Hendrickson, 1988. Originally, *The Humanity of Jesus in the Fourth Gospel.* Philadelphia: Fortress, 1988.

Tovey, Derek. *Narrative Art and Act in the Fourth Gospel.* Journal for the Study of the New Testament: Supplement Series 151. Sheffield: Sheffield Academic Press, 1997.

Troeltsch, Ernst. *The Social Teaching of Christian Churches.* Translated by Olive Wyon. 2 vols. New York: Macmillan, 1932.

Turner, Nigel. *Grammatical Insights into the New Testament.* Edinburgh: T. & T. Clark, 1965.

Van Belle, G. "International Interdisciplinary Seminar on the Fourth Gospel." *Ephemerides theologicae lovanienses* 76 (2000): 216-218.

Van den Bussche, Henri. *Le discours d'adieu de Jésus: Commentaires des chapitres 13 à 17 de l'évangile selon saint Jean.* Tournai: Casterman, 1959.

Vanhoozer, Kevin J. *Is There a Meaning in This Text? The Bible, the Reader, and the Morality of Literary Knowledge.* Grand Rapids, Mich.: Zondervan, 1998.

Wahlde, Urban C. von. "'The Jews' in the Gospel of John: Fifteen Years of Research (1983-1998)." *Ephemerides theologicae lovanienses* 76 (2000): 30-55.

Webber, Robert. *Ancient-Future Faith: Rethinking Evangelicalism for a Postmodern World.* A Bridgepoint Book. Grand Rapids, Mich.: Baker, 1999.

―――. *The Church in the World: Opposition, Tension, or Transformation?* Academie Books. Grand Rapids, Mich.: Zondervan, 1986.

Weber, Max. *The Protestant Ethic and the Spirit of Capitalism.* Translated by Talcott Parsons. London: George Allen & Unwin, 1930.

―――. *The Sociology of Religion.* Translated by Ephraim Fischoff. Boston: Beacon, 1963.

Wells, David F. *No Place for Truth; or, Whatever Happened to Evangelical Theology?* Grand Rapids, Mich.: Eerdmans, 1993.

Wendland, Heinz Dietrich. *Ethik des Neuen Testaments: Eine Einführung.* Grundrisse zum Neuen Testament: Das Neue Testament Deutsch, Ergänzungsreihe 4. Göttingen: Vandenhoeck & Ruprecht, 1970.

Wengst, Klaus. *Bedrängte Gemeinde und verherrlichter Christus: Der historische Ort des Johannesevangeliums als Schlüssel zu seiner Interpretation.* Biblisch-Theologische Studien 5. Neukirchen-Vluyn: Neukirchener Verlag, 1981.

135

Wenham, David. "The Enigma of the Fourth Gospel: Another Look." Pages 102-128 in *Understanding, Studying and Reading.* Edited by Christopher Rowland and Crispin H. T. Fletcher-Louis. Journal for the Study of the New Testament: Supplement Series 153. Sheffield: Sheffield Academic Press, 1998.

Westcott, Brooke Foss. *The Epistles of St John: The Greek Text with Notes.* 3d ed. Grand Rapids, Mich.: Eerdmans, 1966.

"What Is John?" Readers and Readings of the Fourth Gospel. Edited by Fernando F. Segovia. Society of Biblical Literature Symposium Series 3. Atlanta: Scholars Press, 1996.

White, L. Michael. "Shifting Sectarian Boundaries in Early Christianity." *Bulletin of the John Rylands University Library of Manchester* 70 (1988): 7-24.

Williams, Michael Allen. *Rethinking "Gnosticism": An Argument for Dismantling a Dubious Category.* Princeton, N.J.: Princeton University Press, 1996.

Wilson, Bryan R. "An Analysis of Sect Development." *American Sociological Review* 24 (1959): 3-15.

————. *Magic and Millennium: A Sociological Study of Religious Movements of Protest among Tribal and Third-World Peoples.* London: Heinemann, 1973.

————. *Patterns of Sectarianism: Organisation and Ideology in Social and Religious Movements.* London: Heinemann, 1967.

————. *Religion in Sociological Perspective.* Oxford: Oxford University Press, 1982.

————. *Religious Sects.* New York: McGraw-Hill, 1970.

————. *The Social Dimensions of Sectarianism: Sects and New Religious Movements in Contemporary Society.* Oxford: Clarendon, 1990.

————. "A Typology of Sects." Pages 361-383 in *Sociology of Religion: Selected Readings.* Edited by Roland Robertson. New York: Penguin, 1969.

Wilson, Jonathan R. *Living Faithfully in a Fragmented World: Lessons for the Church from MacIntyre's After Virtue.* Christian Mission and Modern Culture. Harrisburg, Pa.: Trinity Press International, 1997.

Winter, J. Alan. *Continuities in the Sociology of Religion: Creed, Congregation and Community.* New York: Harper & Row, 1977.

Witherington III, Ben. *John's Wisdom: A Commentary on the Fourth Gospel.* Louisville, Ky.: Westminster John Knox, 1995.

Wright, N. T. *Jesus and the Victory of God.* Christian Origins and the Question of God 2. Minneapolis: Fortress, 1996.

————. *The New Testament and the People of God.* Christian Origins and the Question of God 1. Minneapolis: Fortress, 1992.

Wuthnow, Robert. *After Heaven: Spirituality in America since the 1950s.* Berkeley: University of California Press, 1998.

Yinger, J. Milton. *The Scientific Study of Religion.* London: Macmillan, 1970.

Yoder, John Howard. "A People in the World: Theological Interpretation." Pages 252-283 in *The Concept of the Believer's Church.* Edited by James Leo Garrett Jr. Scottdale, Pa.: Herald Press, 1969.

―――. *The Priestly Kingdom: Social Ethics as Gospel.* Notre Dame, Ind.: University of Notre Dame Press, 1984.

―――. "Reformation and Missions: A Literature Review." *Occasional Bulletin from the Missionary Research Library* 22/6 (June, 1971): 1-9.

―――. *The Royal Priesthood: Essays Ecclesiological and Ecumenical.* Grand Rapids, Mich.: Eerdmans, 1994.

Young, Amos. "Whither Inclusivism? The Development and Critique of an Evangelical Theology of Religions." *Evangelical Quarterly* 71 (1999): 327-348.

Zimmerman, Mirjam and Ruben. "Der Freund des Bräutigams (Joh 3,29): Deflorations- oder Christuszeuge?" *Zeitschrift für die neutestamentliche Wissenschaft* 90 (1999): 123-130.

Zumstein, Jean. "Le prologue, seuil du Quatrième Évangile." *Recherches de science religieuse* 83 (1995): 217-239.